A SPENDER'S GUIDE TO SAVING

HOW PEOPLE ACROSS THE WORLD ARE USING THESE MODERN METHODS TO SAVE MONEY, INCREASE WEALTH & ACHIEVE FINANCIAL FREEDOM

R. M. MITCHELL

CONTENTS

A GIFT FOR YOU

At MJO Publishing, we believe that can never provide our readers with too much value. All the projects that the other writers and I work on are for the purpose of helping people to improve their lives in one way or another. Therefore, we love to include free, useful gifts in our books to give our readers the best chance to succeed in achieving their goals. Please read on to learn more about your free extra…

When trying to achieve financial stability, as with any long-term goal, it is unrealistic to expect to achieve it overnight. For many people, deciding to stay in their unfavorable situation is much easier than making sacrifices for a better tomorrow. But you are different… You have purchased this book because you have decided that you are ready to make a significant change. Congratulations! However, people are often extremely motivated at the beginning of their journey, but this enthusiasm begins to fade away when they realize they are required to put in the effort.

I understand that this is a part of human nature: very few people enjoy sacrifice. Therefore, I have created a checklist of the most essential pieces of advice for staying motivated. I have researched dozens of helpful tips and tricks to maintaining your enthusiasm, provided by some of the most renowned motivational coaches, and hand-picked the seven that I believe to be the most important for achieving a financial objective. Click here to receive your free checklist or type the following link into your web browser:

https://mjopublisher.activehosted.com/f/1

I have always been a big believer that motivation is the key to success and that it is a concept that we should all understand. Chapter 1 of *A Spender's Guide to Saving* is all about setting your goals. Be sure to receive these seven tips in order to set the targets most suited to you. Nobody should ever set out to achieve a long-term goal without understanding these critical pieces of advice...

Nothing excites me more than hearing the stories of people's journeys to success, no matter their goals! Please feel free to share your story in the review section this book, or share your thoughts, experiences, or questions with me personally via email:

rebecca.mitchell@mjopublishing.com

I wish you the best of luck on your journey to a better financial life; I sincerely hope you enjoy the book!

- *Rebecca Mitchell*

"Every time I swipe my credit card, I feel intensely down. I don't even enjoy myself anymore when I am out with my family." These were the words running through the mind of Charles, an accounting clerk and father of four, when he sat at the kitchen table. His wife, Linda, a stay-at-home mom, was cooking at the time and couldn't help but notice that Charles was profoundly concerned, if not stressed. She asked him, "Charles, what's wrong, my dear?" With not a moment's hesitation, Charles uttered, "Debt, Linda. It's stressing me like hell. I mean, we can't even save for a down payment on a new home for us and the kids. For how long are we going to share this little place with our growing kids? We really need a bigger house."

Charles owed $56,000 in credit card debt, $21,000 more than his family's household annual income. With the minimum payment he was making, it would take 40 years to pay off the debt, as his trusted financial advisor pointed out to him.

Fortunately for Charles, his family, and many other people around the world who face a bleak financial future, there is a solution. And it is found within the pages of this life-altering book, *A Spender's Guide to Saving*. In fact, Charles and his wife resorted to this solution to completely turn their financial life around. In just four years, this loving couple became debt-free. They even had a paid-up mortgage on their recently bought house. Once they became debt-free, this understanding couple began investing in a retirement fund and continued to deposit some of their income into a savings account. You see, the solution worked for Charles and his wife first because they were both tired of having to live from paycheck to paycheck, something I believe haunts you as well. At one stage, one of their children became ill, and they didn't have money to pay the physician to attend to their lovely daughter. I'm sure you wouldn't wish this to happen to anyone. Secondly, they had a dream to buy a new, bigger house to fit the whole family, as their children grew into teenagers.

In this incredible book, I present you with the solution that worked for Charles and his family and many other people around the world. I remember a few years back when I owed $14,000 on my credit card. I had just left a corporate job to pursue my path to attain financial freedom, and I thought entrepreneurship was the way to go. Unfortunately, I didn't have the funds to launch my business idea as powerfully as I had hoped, so things didn't go as planned. I lost everything in a short time and had to resort to using my credit card to help me pay for essentials such as groceries, car repairs, and utilities. I ignored the growing problem of how I would eventually pay off my debt. The bank kept sending notices reminding me to pay because I was hopelessly behind. It felt awful. This forced me to begin a quest to understand how finances, especially debt, really worked. I studied where money comes from and how governments and financial institutions "make money." One of the fantastic books I read is called *Modern Money Mechanics*, released by the Federal Reserve Bank of Chicago. In a short period of this intensive research process, I discovered a common thread to all various debt eradication programs, books, and articles. In fact, I applied just one technique that reduced the interest on my credit card from 22% to 12.5% only by emailing my bank, since I was too afraid to call them.

Learning the story of credit and consumerism was eye-opening. My newfound understanding of how money works and a genuine love for helping other people resulted in the birth of this spectacular book.

According to statista.com, the personal savings rate in the US between June 2015 and February 2020 ranged from about 6% to 9% (Rudden, 2020). There is no doubt that this failure to save is behind the financial stress that blocks many people from enjoying their daily lives. The American Dream remains just that: a distant and unattainable dream for most. But behind this problem lurks the story of debt-fueled by consumerism, the tendency to feel like we do not have enough even if the necessities are taken care of.

The most important discovery that I made in my intense research was that there is a specific sequence to follow to attain financial freedom, save enough for a down payment for a house, or whatever your dream is, even if you're starting with a huge debt.

I've outlined the way to achieve your financial goal in this book.

The process begins with taking the most crucial step to achieve anything of consequence in life. That is to start by clearly specifying what you dream of accomplishing by taking the steps suggested in this book. Your intent may be to buy your own house, get your children to college without taking any loan, taking a month's vacation somewhere far away without incurring debt, or whatever else you may be dreaming about. Perhaps Stephen Covey, author of *The 7 Habits of Highly Successful People*, put it better than I could when he observed, "To begin with the end in mind means to start with a clear under-standing of your destination. It means to know where you're going so that you better understand where you are now and that the steps you take are always in the right direction" (Covey, p.105). I could not agree with Covey more.

Once you know your target, the next step is to understand the role of the mind in handling money. This is what Chapter 2, The Psychology of Money Spending, Saving, and Getting into Debt, is all about. Here's what you'll learn in this chapter:

- What makes people decide to spend money.
- How the brain processes your desire to exchange your hard-earned money for something else.
- Why some people are more inclined to save money while others feel at home with spending it.
- What impact debt has on people, including their financial lives and health.

Chapter 3 goes into detail about debt. Here you'll learn, amongst the many other valuable insights, the following:

- What is debt, and how can it pull you back when you are trying to save your valuable cash?
- Why you should prioritize paying off your debt before you begin your savings plan.
- Why becoming debt-free is essential.

Immediately after discussing debt, we will move on to talking about credit cards in chapter 4. As you already know, credit cards are a massive part of the financial industry, especially personal finance, so it makes absolute sense to explore their advantages and disadvantages. For example, credit cards can be a great resource to help you handle emergencies if appropriately used. We also explore other available avenues to help you deal with unforeseen circumstances if credit cards are not an option for you. However, some of these strategies require tight control, or else they can easily cause irreparable damage. There is a specific situation or condition where credit cards offer the best alternative, but not all forms of credit provide such an advantage, as we will later discuss.

In chapter 5, I show you how to eliminate unnecessary expenses. Yes, in most people's expenses list, some may initially seem unavoidable. But there is a tool you can employ to help you detect precisely those kinds of expenses that you can surprisingly live without. It's a tool that wealthy people use without fail and is a key reason behind their success. Obviously, I cannot tell you what expenses are unnecessary because your life and current situation are unique to you. A payment that I would choose to eliminate may not be appropriate to you. That's why the tool I'm talking about will help you discover what you should spend your money on.

Not all expenses are unnecessary. For example, you

still need to have a roof over your head and must eat every day to survive. However, you may be spending too much on some of these expenses. This is where Chapter 6, How to Reduce the Cost of Your Necessary Spending, becomes so important. In this topic you'll discover the following and more:

- How to identify the areas that you should spend your money on while also reducing the cost.
- How to get your electricity to go further than you currently do. There are other small things you can do that you may be presently ignoring. Don't forget that little things are the makers of big things.

Chapter 7 introduces you to the art of handling the surplus money that you get after reducing costs by following the advice outlined in chapters 5 and 6. In this chapter, you will learn the following:

- How to choose a savings plan that takes your money and moves you further towards your goal.
- A simple technique to ensure you never miss depositing money into your savings plan.

- The right time to begin investing your money.

Often people make deadly financial mistakes when saving. You must become aware of the primary mistakes people make while saving so you can avoid them. In chapter 8, you'll discover the following:

- The kinds of loans that can suck you in with destructive persuasive power if you are desperate for money. The chances of hitting the goal you set for yourself become dangerously close to zero if you get hooked. Most importantly, these kinds of loans trap you into the habit of borrowing money to solve significant problems using a band-aid, which is catastrophic for your long-term financial future.
- The kinds of expenses you should never fail to handle at any cost because you can face some severe consequences. I suggest five ways you can handle these expenses to avoid major financial setbacks.
- The kind of purchases to avoid in order to keep your financial goal on track. Some

people often make this mistake after saving a few dollars over several months.

When you have accumulated the right amount of money in your savings account, it may be an excellent time to start thinking about investing some of it. Most of us are not taught how to invest for one reason or another. But there is no dispute about the value of investing. This can, with care and savvy risk management, become your second income. In chapter 9, I discuss with you how to invest your money. Other things we'll talk about include:

- The benefits of investing. Here we'll talk about investing in products such as mutual funds, shares, bonds, commodities, and other instruments.
- The best strategy for investing. You can easily call this the first rule of successful investing. Some investors get burned because they ignore this important rule.
- The difference between saving and investing.

In chapter 10, we dive into the benefits of staying on top of your finances, even if you feel much more financially secure. Unlike people who struggle financially, the wealthy practice certain habits without fail. In this chapter, we'll discuss the habits that millionaires keep practicing to maintain their financial health in tip-top shape.

Saving can be a pain in the beginning as you alter the way you perceive money and its uses. But if you consider its benefits, you'll find that they far outweigh the short-term inconveniences you may experience. I'm reminded as I write this line about the law of sacrifice, which is a universal law. This law defines sacrifice as giving up something of a smaller value in order to get something of a bigger value. So, to sacrifice is to move to a better station in life. In this case, by sacrificing a little, you become better financially. Here are some of the benefits that occur to people who save:

- Savings can help you handle emergencies like urgent car repairs much better.
- Savings provide a cushion for when you lose your job unexpectedly.
- Savings can finance significant purchases like vacations.
- Best of all, you'll find a lot of stress gets lifted off your shoulders.

As you can see, having a savings account can be a literal lifesaver. I've yet to meet anyone who followed the principles discussed in this book and failed to ace their financial goal(s). I don't see how you could lose by saving your hard-earned money instead of giving it to others while you deal with stress that hurts your health. The time to begin saving was yesterday, but the second-best time is today. The reason is simple. The longer you wait, the longer you'll stay in the current financial situation that's hurting you month after month. Also, you may be delaying accruing enough interest on your savings and retirement funds. So, move off the fence, study and implement the process outlined in this manual and put your finances on the right track.

Let me offer words by one of the most prolific men who ever graced the face of the earth, Leonardo da Vinci, the Italian master painter, sculptor, and engineer. He said, "I have been impressed with the urgency of doing. Knowing is not enough; we must apply. Being willing is not enough; we must do."

And this action for you begins with the next chapter, The Power of Starting with the End in Mind.

1

THE POWER OF STARTING WITH THE END IN MIND

Sophia and Owen, a couple, were on a winter vacation with their friend, Liam. They thoroughly enjoyed skiing every other day. Each night they sat beside a nice, warm fire and listened to personal development audiobooks. While listening, they'd sometimes stop the audio and discuss the lessons they had heard. At some point, Liam suddenly stopped the audiobook and asked Owen, "So what's your plan for the next year?" This question caught Owen by surprise. After a moment's hesitation, he replied, "Well, Sophia and I would like to build an emergency fund to cover six months of our monthly expenses." "Oh, that's great," said Liam, shyly looking at Owen. Immediately, he remembered that Owen had said the same thing the previous year. So, he went on and asked, "But, isn't that what you said you wanted to do during our last winter vacation? Are you telling me that it never happened? What's going to be different this time?" Owen felt quite ashamed to admit that both he and his wife had never actually begun saving towards their emergency fund.

This is what I want to talk about in this chapter. You see, there's a way to set goals that improves your chances of achieving them. Unfortunately, most people overlook the essential elements to include in goal setting. Not surprisingly, many people are pumped up at the start but soon give up. It's more like what people do when they set New Year's resolutions. They get excited in the beginning, but soon the fire they had in their bellies die out, for most, in less than six months. Let me set the stage by talking to you about recent research on goal-setting.

This research was published in the *Journal of Contemporary Educational Psychology* in November 2019. The study scientists, Schippers et al., wanted to investigate the relationship between goal-setting and academic performance. To that end, they studied 2,934 first-year university students from four successive intakes. The first and second first-year cohort were the control group (that is, they did not participate in the goal-setting intervention), while the third and fourth cohorts actively participated. The researchers knew that goal setting was effective on things like job performance but wanted to have empirical findings, especially in the education setting.

Their approach consisted of four stages. The first stage required the participating students to detail their ideal future and list their personal values. In the second stage, these students were tasked with coming up with detailed plans on achieving their ideal prospects and values. And the third stage required the participants to publicize their commitment to their goals. The results showed that 89% of students from cohort one completed all the three steps, while in group two, 91%.

After analyzing their data and the academic transcripts of all the students, researchers found that those who participated in the goal-setting process scored 20% higher academically than the control group. You would have thought that the type of goals you set would influence whether you achieve a goal or not. Not so. The researchers discovered, to their shock, that the kind of goals the students set for themselves did not affect performance. What mattered was writing personal goals and specifying a plan to achieve them. The scientists concluded, "It is the process of choosing and writing about personal goals and how to achieve them, rather than the inclusion of specifically academic versus non-academic goals, that is related to academic performance" (Schippers et al., 2019, p. 8).

This conclusion has a bearing on how you should set your personal goals. But why did the goal-setting model improve the participating students' results? To answer that question, we should talk about goal-setting and your brain.

YOUR BRAIN AND GOAL-SETTING

I won't talk about the details of your whole brain. I'll touch on the functions of the significant parts of the brain and spend a bit more time on the role that influences goal-setting the most. Have you ever wondered why you desire to make a change and actually find it hard to stick to the change? It's commendable to want to change your behavior because if it doesn't change, your financial results will stay as they are. But the most important thing you should realize is that you are 100% responsible for making the change.

To make that change, it is necessary to know how your brain functions. The human brain consists of the brain stem, midbrain, and cortex. This major organ is further divided into two major sections, the right, and the left brains. The brainstem is responsible for the fight or flight response when stimulated. The midbrain is the emotional center and houses the amygdala, which allows or blocks fear signals to the prefrontal cortex (the thinking center). The cortex carries out high executive functions such as decision-making. The left-side of the brain is responsible for tasks such as analyzing and logic, while the right brain is home to the imagination and creativity.

For goal setting to work, you must align all the brain parts. If not, then the chances are that your goal won't see the light of the day. To align all these brain parts, it is vital to speak the language of each of these centers. I want you to recognize that your brain is a pattern and pleasure-seeking device. As such, it is always looking for ways to help you materialize your desires. If you have been getting financial results that you don't want, the chances are that your brain has been focusing on someone else's goals.

In the brain, there is a sensory filter called the reticulating activating system (RAS). Its job is to simplify our lives by automating a lot of what we do. A mechanical filter has holes that only allow particles of specific sizes to pass through. Any particle larger than the holes gets blocked. The RAS works on that principle. What it does is allow only certain information to reach the cortex for processing. At the same time, it ensures that some actions (like blinking to protect eyes from a splinter) are acted upon immediately. Most, if not all, of the information that reaches RAS comes from the five senses (hearing, sight, touch, smell, and taste).

Now, the goals you set will be new to your RAS and the brain. So, RAS may block them from reaching the cortex for further processing and acceptance. To improve the chances of making your goals a reality, there are some things you'll do. The students who skyrocketed their academic performance did some of those things, like writing their goals down. When you write your goals down, you involve your sight, feelings, and also think about them. In addition, if you plan, as the students did, you trigger your imagination (right brain), which can also activate your emotions.

Are you afraid of snakes, heights, spiders, dogs, loud

noises, or darkness? If not, what are you afraid of? Now, take 20 seconds to think about what you fear. If it's a snake, think about the kind of snake you fear. What does it look like? What's its color? How long is it? Now, how do you feel in your body? Is your heart rate regular? Of course, it increases. That's the power of visualization. Your brain cannot distinguish between what's real from what's fictitious. So, you're going to take advantage of the nature of your brain to set financial goals.

HOW TO SET YOUR FINANCIAL GOALS

Your financial goals will help you make quick decisions. Most importantly, they'll show you the progress you're making as you act on them. One overlooked function of your goals is that they help you figure out quickly how to get to where you want. The goals you'll come up with will all follow the SMARTER formula. This formula simply states that your goals should be specific, measurable, achievable, realistic, time-focused, ethical, and rewarding. Here's a seven-step method to set winning financial goals:

1. Write down a list of all your wants and needs on

two separate sheets of paper. If you wish, you may only write down needs.

2. Prioritize your needs and wants based on how much you desire each. Focus more of your time on your needs than your desires. Now, select six to eight of your most important goals. As you prioritize your needs and wants, consider answering these four vital questions for each:

Why is the need or want essential?

Why is the answer you gave above so important to you?

What are the consequences for you of not achieving the need or want you chose above?

Would the consequences above worry you? If so, why?

3. Now, assign the time frame for achieving each of the selected goals. Some of your goals will be short-term (less than five years), intermediate (between five and ten years), or long-term (over ten years).

4. Work out how much it would cost you to pay for your goal today. From this number, figure out the monthly savings you'll need to make to hit your target. This then becomes your financial goal. If you did this exercise correctly, each of your financial goals should be SMARTER. You don't stop here. Just

listing your goals is good, but it's not an effective way of achieving them. This next step is vital.

5. Write down all your goals on a clean sheet of paper. Make three copies of this paper and stick one copy in every one of the three rooms in your home that you frequent the most like the kitchen, bedroom, etc. The print in the kitchen helps you publicize your goals and improves your chances of achieving it, as you saw with the students in the study above. Keep one sheet with you, preferably in your purse, and read it anytime during the day.

6. Read your goal sheet every night just before you sleep and immediately as you awake in the morning. These are the times when your mind can be easily influenced.

7. Now, break down each of your goals into steps you must take to achieve it. This step forces you to plan how to achieve your goal. It matches the second stage the students did in the goal-setting research we talked about earlier.

Some people believe in getting an accountability partner so that they push themselves to follow through. If you feel that's something that can help you, go ahead and find one.

2

THE PSYCHOLOGY OF MONEY SPENDING, SAVING AND GETTING INTO DEBT

D id you know? US citizens are drowning in consumer debt. According to America's Debt Help Organization, in the second quarter of 2019, the total consumer debt was a mind-numbing $13.86 trillion, an increase of $209 million from the previous quarter. A staggering 189 million of the US population own a credit card. As a matter of fact, the average household carries at least four credit cards. Most of the consumer debt falls into one or more of the following categories: mortgages, cars, student loans, and credit cards. The latter contributes to almost a third of this debt at 26%, and the average household owes about $8,398 in credit card debt (www.debt.org, n.d.).

You would think this data may be unique to the

United States of America. In my search for the truth about money and debt, I discovered some South African debt data that astounded me. For example, at the end of December 2017, there were 25.31 million credit-active consumers on the credit bureaus' records registered with the South African National Credit Regulator. At the same time, the total debt owed to various financial institutions amounted to ZAR1.76 trillion ($134.35 billion at an exchange rate of $1 = ZAR13.10) (National Credit Regulator Annual Report, 2018). Even more surprising, I found this statement by the South African Reserve Bank (SARB): "A sustained improvement in consumer demand and business confidence is needed to boost corporate demand for credit. Encouragingly, credit extension to the household sector inched higher from 3.7% in January 2018 to 5.7% in December and grew by 4.6% on average in 2018 compared to only 2.6% in 2017 and 2.3% in 2016" (Quarterly Bulletin No. 291, 2019, p.53). It's pretty clear that SARB wants the population to take as much credit as is possible, hence the excitement when credit extension to households increased.

There is no argument that debt is a leading issue enveloping both developed and developing countries. The question is, why do we succumb to debt?

To answer this question, we need to look at two major types of consumers, spenders and savers.

THE TWO KINDS OF CONSUMERS

There are two major kinds of consumers in the market, the spenders and the savers. Which are you? Before we answer that question, let's talk about what happens in the brain moments before a person buys something.

Gerhard Raab, from the Ludwigshafen University of Applied Science, together with a team of researchers, wanted to investigate the difference between compulsive and non-compulsive buyers during purchase decision-making. Their study, published in 2011 in the *Journal of Consumer Policy*, looked at the buying behavior of 49 women, with 23 compulsive and 26 non-compulsive using functional Magnetic Resonance Imaging (fMRI) for brain scanning. They found that the compulsive buyers had higher brain activity in the nucleus accumbens than the non-compulsive purchasers. The nucleus accumbens shows higher activity when you desire a particular product. On the other hand, the compulsive shoppers showed lower activity in the insula than the non-compulsive buyers. The insula's activity level indicates the level of negative arousal to buying. This study, by itself, doesn't tell you what to do to improve the activation of the insula if you are a compulsive spender. We'll talk about what to do to neutralize your impulsive spending behavior in a moment.

Researchers have been interested in the behavior of spenders and savers to figure out how they deal with financial decision making. For example, a 2007 study by Scott Rick, Associate Professor of Marketing at the University of Michigan's Ross School of Business, and his team of researchers looked at the difference in spenders and savers' experience when paying for an item. They believed the results could be used as a reliable predictor of credit card debt and savings. In this study, reported in the *Journal of Consumer Research* in 2008, the researchers asked participants if they would be willing to pay a hypothetical fee for overnight delivery of a gift for completing a survey. The charge was either stated as a "small" $5 or just $5. In the "small" $5 category, there were 295 participants, while the number of participants in the other group was 243. Results that came though were interesting as shown in the figure below:

PROPORTION WILLING TO PAY FEE (STUDY 1)

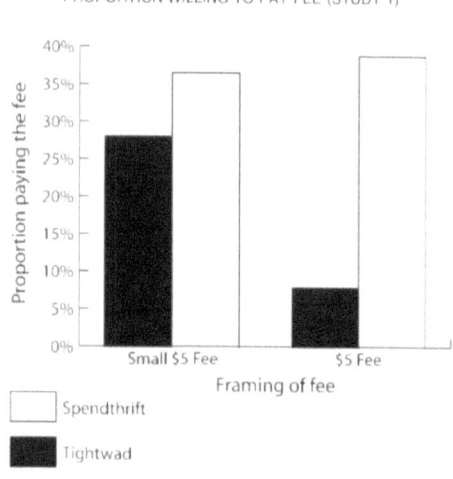

Figure 1: Research results of the buying
behaviors of spenders and savers

As you can see, there is no significant difference in response by the spendthrifts whether the fee is quoted as a "small" $5 or only as a $5 fee. However, the savers (tightwads) are extremely sensitive to the framing of the fee. It's quite interesting that both the savers and spenders responded almost the same way when the word "small" was used to frame the $5. The researchers suggested that this frame mitigated the pain of paying. You probably are wondering why people could behave so differently to the same stimulus? We'll answer that question in a short while. Let's first dive into another study on materialism.

In this study, Kirk Warren from the Department of Psychology, Virginia Commonwealth University, and a team of researchers wanted to investigate if people who differ in materialism level behave differently in their day-to-day spending. They also wanted to figure out if these people experienced different emotions as a result of their purchases. This study was run over a 3-week period and involved 74 participants. The researchers tracked the spending behavior of the participants.

The results were not unexpected. People with high levels of materialism made more discretionary buying decisions and paid more cash on necessities than people low in materialism. Interestingly, they found that the level of income did not affect buying decisions. Perhaps it is a surprise that highly materialistic people reported elevated levels of "buyer's letdown." This means that once the high materialists bought an item, they didn't experience a pleasant emotional experience. The conclusion these experts arrived at was that high materialism is strongly correlated with poor money management skills and impulsive buying. And this is why highly materialistic people tend to have higher levels of debt than low materialists. In this paper, published in the *Journal of Happiness Studies* in 2015, these experts reviewed other studies that proved that materialistic teenagers enjoy shopping, save less, and have an elevated desire for new products.

Based on the two studies discussed above, we can conclude that people with high materialism tend to be spenders. The latter, as we have seen, is more likely to be trapped in debt. It is widely known that personal debt is an excellent measurer of depression, mental disorders, psychological stress, and suicidal thoughts and behavior. Elizabeth Sweet and her colleagues from the Northwestern University Feinberg School of Medicine carried out a study to figure out the impact of financial debt on psychological and general health. In the research, reported in August 2013 in the *Journal of Social Science*, these scientists studied 8,400 young adults between the ages of 24 and 32 using data collected over 15 years by the National Longitudinal Study of Adolescent Health. As expected, the researchers concluded that household debt is an independent predictor of general health and psychological stress.

You may have heard about the study of America's millionaires by Thomas Stanley, Ph.D. and William Danko, Ph.D. The results of their extensive study are detailed in their book *The Millionaire Next Door*. In their book, this is what a typical millionaire looks like. "I am a tightwad. That's one of the main reasons I completed a long questionnaire for a crispy $1 bill. Why else would I spend two or three hours being personally interviewed by these authors? They paid me $100, $200, or $250. Oh, they made me another offer to donate in my name the money I earned from my interview to my favorite charity. But I told them, "I am my favorite charity"(Danko & Stanley, 1996, p.11)." This underlines the importance of having the attributes of a saver if you want to get ahead financially. Not only will these habits help you achieve your financial goals, but they'll also move you further away from the stressful debt.

THE REAL CAUSE OF PEOPLE'S MONEY HABITS

Every person has a self-image about money. Some people call this your money blueprint. Essentially, this image is your views on money, and it affects how you use cash. Sometimes I ask people close to me what they think money is. Most of them believe that money is the paper or coins to exchange goods and services with. This definition of money is totally off the mark. If we ask, "Where does money come from?" we quickly realize that what we think of as money is not real money. Money is simply a tool that represents the value of goods and services. And the worth of products and services is determined by the parties involved in the exchange process. For example, a person who values this book highly may pay $200 for it while someone who appreciates it far less may want to have it for free. Notice that the perception of value does not change the nature of this book.

The big question to ask is, "what determines a person's perspective on value?" This is another way of asking, "What makes someone an impulsive buyer while another pays due consideration to their purchase decisions?" Our self-image of money is behind most of our views. Where does this self-image come from? To answer that question, let's visit with Maxwell Maltz, a plastic surgeon and author of *Psycho-Cybernetics*.

Maltz was astounded when he discovered that after reconstructing some of his patients' faces, their lives immediately changed for the better. However, some remained unchanged and left this astute plastic surgeon wondering why people could respond so differently to the same experience. He went on a quest to find the reason why some of his patients started enjoying their lives immediately after undergoing surgery. In contrast, others continued to live as if nothing had happened. The answer, he discovered, lay in the self-image concept: your own view of who you are. But where does this self-image come from? There are many sources. But there is no arguing that most of it was formed when you and I were children. In Maltz's words, "Your hidden self-image was formed when you were still a child. At that time, it formed a picture of what your lot in life should be. Since then, you have changed, but it has not. It holds the same plans for you it formed in your childhood, and it influences your mind to achieve the plans it wants, not the goals and desires you really want" (Maltz, 2010, p. iv). What does this mean for you in relation to money? Simply that, whether you are a spender or saver is a result of influences you were exposed to while you were a child.

As Maltz suggests, if your ways of handling money are to change, this means changing your self-image about money. I'm sure you're already wondering, "How do I change my self-image about money?" That's a great and necessary question, and it is at the core of tweaking your ways of handling money. It starts with understanding how your subconscious mind works because it houses your self-image. The beautiful thing is that this part of the mind can be influenced. The technique to use is called self-suggestion. It is used to replace thoughts and habits with new ones, hopefully, beneficial ones. It's a great tool to use to write your new money blueprint in your subconscious. Here are words to impress in your mind over and over to build a healthy mindset about money:

"Money is continually circulating in my life. I am excited to release it, and it returns to me multiplied in amazing ways. I love money; I like it, I use it intelligently and in a useful way. Bundles of money flow to me in abundance, and I use it for good only. I am grateful and excited for my good and the wealth of my subconscious mind."

Read these self-image-altering words in a relaxed and calm manner. This works exceedingly well if done early in the morning and just before you go to sleep at night because, during those times, the gate-keeper of the subconscious mind (the conscious mind) drops its guard. While doing this, it is vital to begin building new habits that support your attempts to become a money saver.

HOW TO BUILD NEW MONEY HABITS

Habits are nothing but routine and automatic ways of behaving. A collection of practices is commonly called a paradigm, hence the use of the term paradigm shift when making significant changes. If saving money is a challenge to you, the chances are that some of your habits are destructive. To change them, you must first become aware that they exist. That requires you to take inventory of yourself to discover your habitual way of handling money. Here are a few questions to think about and write their solutions:

- How do you react when you see an advertisement for a desirable television, home theatre system, fridge, or a piece of clothing, or smell delicious food in the mall?
- How do you usually behave when it's payday?
- How do you usually make your purchases and when?
- Are you in the habit of buying using cash or credit? Why? What triggers you to buy something on credit?
- Do you save money regularly? If not, why?

- Do you often buy things to impress someone? Why do you do that?

There are many more questions you can ask yourself about money to bring your hidden money habits to the surface and then deal with them.

If you carefully observe how you behave in any one of the situations I mentioned above, you would have taken an enormous step towards obliterating lousy money habits. To alter a habit, you need a trigger and some form of an incentive or a reward. Let's say your typical response to smelling excellent food in the mall is to crave and then buy it. In other words, the smell of food triggers the action of buying to satisfy your craving. How would you break this habit? Clearly, you cannot remove the trigger (the smell of the food), but you can change what you do to satisfy your craving still. For example, you can drink free water to stop the craving or turn your attention to something that excites you without a cost. In other words, you simply turn your attention from food to something that would still help avoid buying the food while satisfying the craving.

The model sounds extremely simple, and it is. However, to turn your response to the smell of food and craving into a habit requires the overlooked law of learning that I've come to call the law of repetition. Remember the Russian psychologist Pavlov and his experiment with dogs? If you've never heard of him and his experiments, let me give you a short introduction to the study. Pavlov rang a bell and immediately after, gave his dogs some food. He repeated this process several times until eventually, he simply rang the bell and the dogs salivated even if Pavlov didn't have food in his hands. In other words, the dogs associated the ringing bell with eating such that merely ringing the bell triggered an automatic response.

WHY YOU SHOULD PRIORITIZE PAYING OFF YOUR DEBT

Living from paycheck to paycheck is like literally skating on thin ice. James, a 32-year-old train conductor, habitually made day-to-day purchases with his credit card. Over time he began to battle to pay it off. Murphy's Law happened to him. Murphy's Law states if something can go wrong, it *will* go wrong. He was laid off from the job that he loved, and his life with Talitha, his wife of 4 years, took a knock. They began to struggle. Their credit card issuer sent them notice after notice to remind them to pay. It was stressful, indeed. Luckily James eventually landed a new job, and he and his wife resolved to get rid of their credit card debt.

It was not easy in the beginning as they had to take

ownership of their finances and learn to communicate effectively as a couple. But today, this couple is debt-free primarily due to the formula I'll share with you below in a moment.

Life is unpredictable. When you are living from paycheck to paycheck, emergencies can hit. You may need urgent car or house repairs. Perhaps, like James, you may be laid off without warning. How would you survive? It's unlikely that when this situation kicks in, you have a healthy savings account. One of the most significant contributors to living paycheck to paycheck is debt.

Let me make an important point before I continue. What I'll talk about from here onwards is so relevant and helpful whether you have debt or not. If you have debt, this information is critical, while if you have no debt, you'll learn about its dangers and advantages.

Debt, by definition, is money that you owe to someone else, and usually, it is returned with interest. There are two common kinds of debt, secured or unsecured debt. A secured debt is a kind where an asset is used as a backup in the event you fail to make payments. Essentially, your creditor will repossess the asset as payment for the debt. Great examples of secured loans are mortgages and some car loans.

In contrast, unsecured debt is not backed up by collateral. One of the most common unsecured debts used in our time is credit card debt. Let me show you how you can pay off your debt the fastest way possible.

THE QUICKEST WAY TO PAY OFF YOUR DEBT

It does not matter what kind of debt you may have. The quickest way to pay off all your debt is by paying more than the minimum amount of money required. Now, how do you do it if you are living paycheck to paycheck? The answer is that you must create a surplus. How do you do that? There are many ways, and let's consider a few easy and quick ones below. Here's something fundamental before learning how to create a surplus.

The debt eradication formula I want to share with you works very well if you take this very first step exceedingly seriously: freeze your habit of accumulating debt. This step is probably the most challenging for most of us, but it must be done. Think about this for a moment. When you're in a hole, and you want to come out, do you keep digging further? Of course not. What you do instead is figure out a way to come out of the hole, isn't it? You may say that you regularly use your credit card to pay for essentials like groceries. No problem, keep doing so. However, make this small change. Simply use your credit card as a debit card. This means that after buying with the credit card, ensure you pay all the money into your credit card account before interest is added. Do this every month without fail. It will also be useful for your credit score.

HOW TO GENERATE SURPLUS MONEY ON A MONTHLY BASIS

There are many overlooked ways you can use to create surplus money to supplement your minimum monthly payment on your debt. In other words, the idea is to create another income stream solely for the purpose of helping you annihilate your liabilities quicker.

Create a Side Hustle

Here's a simple process to follow to discover what kind of income stream you can add easily:

- First, answer each of the following questions to identify your skills and talents. Remember that talent means anything you naturally find easy to do or even to learn.
- What topics do you like reading about most of the time? Allen Cheng started by summarizing the books he read to make them easy to use. Now, he has created a company that produces unique book summaries for his customers. Don't underestimate what you like reading because there may be an opportunity lurking in there.
- Do you have activities you like doing outside of work? If so, what are they?
- What are the activities you do well without seeking anyone's help?
- What activities do you often do outside of work?
- What topic do you find you enjoy talking about or even guide others on?

The questions above help you quickly discover some of your overlooked talents and skills. Believe it or not, your abilities and skills are the sources from which you can start making serious headway into paying your debt fast.

- Secondly, go to your favorite search engine and type in a keyword about your skill. For example, if you like talking about the power of memory, you can type in "How to improve memory?" in your search engine. I did this exercise and found that other people ask questions like these:
- How can I improve my memory fast?
- How can I improve my memory and concentration?
- Why is my memory so bad?
- What can I take to improve my memory?

What this short exercise does is tell me some people want to improve their memory. So, if I have the skill or talent, I can help these people.

The other option is to go to forums and type the same keyword. A quick search landed me on a forum called Art of Memory. So, this appears to be a good idea to pursue. Once you are satisfied that there is a market for your plan, you can go ahead and figure out how to help the market. There are a few ways to do this.

- **You can teach the market**. Teaching does not necessarily require a specialized qualification. Yes, perhaps to teach in a school it does. But for our intentions, this is unnecessary and can even be a disadvantage. Teaching simply means sharing what you know with people who want to learn. You can offer private or group classes in almost any topic you wish to, such as music, gardening, math, writing, and so on. Demand for learning another language will never cease to exist. If English is your second language or you can speak another language fluently, why not become a language tutor? Many online programs give you all the training you need to tutor students.
- **You can consult with companies**. There are companies that can do with the improvement of their employees. If you are a great merchandiser, you can offer your services to such companies, and they'll pay

you for it. Some people even go on to quit their job when such side hustles bring in big money.

- **You can become a freelancer.** There are websites like Guru, Freelancer, PeoplePerHour, Upwork, and many others that connect freelancers with companies and people who require a variety of services. The work available on these sites ranges from writing, typing, editing, proofreading, marketing, copywriting, and many others.

- **You can create and sell digital products.** This is really one of the simplest things to do. All it requires is a product such as an eBook, audiobook, or video lessons that you can promote on sites like Clickbank or your own simple website. Books for young children are often straightforward and cheap to produce. However, you still need to be able to promote your product for you to earn from them.

Another possible way of adding an income stream involves getting a part-time job if you can spare a few hours per week.

Negotiate Lower Interest Rates on Applicable Monthly Bills

Did you know that you can negotiate almost anything that involves the interaction of people? Yes, you can. There are certain monthly bills that are nearly a given to negotiate lower payment rates or interest rates. But most of us have forgotten the negotiating skill that we used so well when we were children. There is no better time to reignite this skill than when you want to pay off your debt quickly. Below I'll share with you six kinds of bills on which you stand a good chance of paying less than you currently do. Thereafter, I'll take you through a case study to show you how it works in real life.

- **Satellite or cable television**: the providers of satellite or cable television face stiff competition from one another. This is a perfect thing for you because most of these companies are willing to negotiate with their customers. They would rather keep their current, reliable customers than try to get new ones. Also, it is cheaper to do business with existing customers than looking for new business. What you do is call your satellite or cable TV provider and state your case. If you discover that the company doesn't want to budge, suggest that you have found better offers somewhere and are willing to walk away. Typically they'll consider your proposal. If they don't, simply move over to another provider who gives you a better monthly subscription.

- **Internet service**: this service is also crowded with providers. You can approach them the same way you negotiated with the satellite TV provider.

- **Credit card interest rate**: are you currently paying what you consider high-interest rates? There is a way to get better annual percentage rates (APR). Shop around for better interest rates online. Once you discover a few good ones, give your current card issuer a call and let them know that you would like a better interest rate than they currently offer you. This is your best bet because it can free a few dollars monthly to settle your debt quickly.

- **Car insurance rates**: This category is also very competitive, so it allows you the opportunity to negotiate. First, you should shop around for good deals and terms that are favorable. Then, call your car insurer and ask for an improved interest rate. Some other options to consider include bundling your rent or homeowner's insurance with car insurance with the same insurer. In some cases, a review of your current terms may reveal some items, such as a rental car that you may not need, provided you have a second car. Doing this may lower your monthly car insurance premium.

- **Monthly rent payments**: This option works great if you are reliable and have a good record of paying. It is cheaper and less of a hassle to keep a reliable tenant than opting for someone who may turn out to be troublesome. Negotiate for a better deal when you renew your lease. Be willing to sign a longer lease if your landlord is willing to reduce the monthly payment.

Those are just a few of the possible ideas you may pursue to free or create extra cash you can use to increase the minimum payment on your debt. They are not, by all means, a complete list. Some other options may include refinancing your home for a lower interest rate if it mathematically and financially makes sense. Importantly, no one prevents you from implementing all of the ideas suggested above. Warning: don't just use the extra money you get haphazardly. Let me show how best to use it with an example.

How to Use Surplus Cash to Pay Off Your Debt Faster

Congratulations. You now have extra cash to accelerate paying off your debt. It is now time to carry on the process I introduced at the beginning of this chapter.

1. Make a list of all the debt that you have.
2. For each of the debt recorded above, make four columns and do the following:

- Write the total amount you owe.
- Write the minimum monthly payment you must make to remain in good standing.
- Write the interest rate the financial institution charges you.
- Work out the number of months it could take to pay off the debt.

A spreadsheet helps with the calculation, and I used one in the following example.

1. Rank the order of your debt in descending order (from smallest to largest according to the amount of debt you owe).

An example:

Debt situation before payment optimization			
	Credit card	**Personal Loan**	**Car Loan**
Remaining balance	$5,000	$15,000	$16,000
Interest rate	19.50%	5.99%	4.42%
Number of payments remaining (months)	36	60	60
Minimum monthly payment	$184.55	$289.92	$297.71

Table 1: Debt arranged from smallest to largest

Now, let's begin to learn how to use the surplus you generate.

Let's consider a situation where Mia, a 34-year-old single woman who has two kids, has the following debts:

- A credit card debt of $5,000
- A personal loan of $15,000.

- A car loan of $16,000.

In summary, this is how Mia's debt situation looks like before adding surplus cash she managed to generate:

Debt situation before payment optimization			
	Credit card	Personal Loan	Car Loan
Remaining balance	$5,000	$15,000	$16,000
Interest rate	19.50%	5.99%	4.42%
Number of payments remaining (months)	36	60	60
Minimum monthly payment	$184.55	$289.92	$297.71

Table 2: Mia's debt situation before beginning the process of paying it off quicker

The first debt to pay off will be her credit card because it is the smallest of the three. The reason we start with the lower debt is that she can get quick wins and become more motivated to continue.

How to Settle a $5,000 Credit Card Debt in Only 16 Months

Let me emphasize: the process we are going to follow applies to any kind of debt. Mia's income equals her expenses, meaning that she lives from paycheck to paycheck. So, there's no extra money available for her to pay her debts quicker.

So, Mia must first "create" extra cash. And she can

do it. There are two overlooked opportunities she can take advantage of, namely, the interest rate on her car loan and the insurance premium.

Here are the payments Mia currently makes:

Monthly payments without optimization	
Monthly repayments	$297.42
Monthly car insurance	$129.00
Total monthly payment	$426.42

Table 3: Mia's Car payments before making changes

But before she can take advantage of those opportunities, there's something she needs to understand about financial institutions and insurance companies. The main interest of banks and other financial institutions is to make as much money as they can. So, the more customers they have, the better for them. Additionally, they don't want to ever lose their customers to competitors. As such, they try as best as they can to keep their regular buyers.

How to Create Extra Cash from Car Financing

All Mia needs to do is call the financial institution that financed her car and tell them that she wants to pay off her car loan aggressively. She continues and tells her financier that, unfortunately, she does not have extra cash to do so. Then she suggests to the financier to offer her a better interest rate. This is part of a strategy called negotiating – it is what debt consolidators do on your behalf if you take their services. It is a skill that children are very good at, but most adults ignore or overlook it.

The bank will usually not like this because they stand to lose on the interest amount and possibly bank fees. No problem if they say to her, "No, we can't." Because she can now take advantage of the bank's greediness. What she does is tell them that she has gotten a few quotations with several car financiers, and they are offering her 0.5% to 1.5% lower interest rate than them.

She continues and asks them what best interest rate can they offer her and then keeps quiet until they respond. If they don't offer her what she wants, she simply reminds them, "Remember I've been banking with you for over six years. I wouldn't like to switch my balance over to another financier." And then keep quiet. At this point, the bank usually would balk... and consider her proposal.

Why? Because financial institutions hate losing clients to their competitors. Also, the banks and other financiers are in the business of making money. Why then would they choose to lose money?

And thus, our friend could get her interest reduced to say 2.88%. And now, her monthly car payment becomes $286.65, excluding insurance.

Monthly payments without optimization		Reduced by
Monthly repayments	$286.65	3.62%
Monthly car insurance	$129.00	0.00%
Total monthly payment	$415.65	2.53%

Table 4: Mia's car payments after reduction of her financing interest rate

This means that she now saves $10.77 every month compared to before improving her car financing situation. This may not look like much. Wait 'til you see just now what impact this "little" money can have on your financial life. Let's add this $10.77 to Mia's minimum payment on her credit card and see what the numbers say. That little money reduces the time Mia would take to pay off her credit from 36 months to 33 months without her adding any of her extra money.

Credit Card					
Remaining balance	Interest rate	Number of payments remaining (months)	Minimum monthly payment	Optimization payment	Total monthly payment
$5,000	19.50%	33	$184.55	$10.77	$195.32

Table 5: Impact of the increased monthly payment on Mia's credit card repayment period

It's exciting, isn't it? If you were to do this with all your debt, how would it make you feel? Ecstatic, right?

Let's now see the impact of making changes to her car insurance on the time it takes for Mia to pay off her credit card.

How to "Create" Money Using Car Insurance

The principle is very similar to the first one we did above. Just follow what we did in lowering interest rates above. There is also a second, more comfortable option. Mia could simply go online to websites such as **www.quotelab.com** and ask for car insurance quotes for her vehicle. Remember that car insurance is what is called short-term insurance. So you can change it a number of times, say two or three times a year. But I would suggest changing car insurers perhaps twice a year to keep your name (and brand) respectable. Immediately **www.quote-**

lab.com will bring quotation results from several top national and local car insurance companies.

All Mia does is choose the insurance that offers a lower premium for the same kind of cover as before. However, she should be careful of the small print that may hide important clauses. They tend to be very different from company to company. Let's say Mia gets a new insurance premium of $115. How will this change her total monthly car payments? Here's the new, improved situation:

Monthly payments without optimization		Reduced by
Monthly repayments	$286.65	3.62%
Monthly car insurance	$115.00	10.85%
Total monthly payment	$401.65	5.81%

Table 6: Mia's total car repayments after reduction of her insurance premium

Reducing her car insurance premium would free a total of $24.77 monthly that Mia could use as she pleases. But there's a better way to use this cash. What if she adds it to her monthly payment of the credit card debt? Let's see how her situation will change. If she does, she'll pay off her credit card in 30 months, instead of the original 36. This means she saves herself an extra six months of stress. I'm sure she would feel lighter.

Credit Card					
Remaining balance	Interest rate	Number of payments remaining (months)	Minimum monthly payment	Optimization payment	Total monthly payment
$5,000	19.50%	30	$184.55	$24.77	$209.32

Table 7: Reduction of payment period on credit card debt

It is amazing what happens when you look at financial matters from a different point of view. This exercise has demonstrated two critical ideas:

1. It's vital for us to do calculations before making major financial decisions. Most of us don't do this, and it can be costly! We tend to make emotional decisions and, in the long run, land ourselves in unnecessary financial trouble. So, the next time you want to make a significant financial decision, do the necessary financial calculations beforehand.

2. We need to take a lot more responsibility when it comes to our financial matters. I mean... who cares about our finances more than we do?

Now, we have seen how Mia saved herself six months on paying her credit card debt. This means she saved herself the monthly stress of paying off her credit card debt. Next, we'll see what Mia can do with the extra cash she now has after paying off her credit card. It's actually effortless, you know.

Mia's advantage is that she has now developed the habit (a good habit) of paying off her debts quicker. She has now also developed the habit of living without this extra money. So, instead of buying a new cell phone or a new pair of jeans, she can simply roll her extra cash into paying off her personal loan. But how? Let's see.

Just by doing this, she will have paid up her personal loan in 47 months (saving herself 13 full months of stress and added interest).

Personal Loan					
Remaining balance	Interest rate	Number of payments remaining (months)	Minimum monthly payment	Optimization payment	Total monthly payment
$8,059.13	5.99%	17	$289.92	$209.32	$499.24

Table 8: Quicker payment of personal loan after increasing repayments

Don't forget that interest is money a financier gets for loaning you money. The quicker you finish paying off the loan, the less interest you pay. Mia's savings exclude bank fees and service fees if they're applicable. What's next then for Mia? Once the personal loan is paid off, she now attacks the car loan. Mia now has $499.24 extra ($24.77 + $184.55 + $289.92) available to add to her car monthly instalment. All she does is again roll this money into paying off her car loan, and the situation improves like this. She saves herself eight months of paying the stress-causing debt.

Car Loan					
Remaining balance	Interest rate	Number of payments remaining (months)	Minimum monthly payment	Optimization payment	Total monthly payment
$3,772.21	4.42%	5	$297.71	$499.24	$796.94

Table 9: Faster car repayment after increasing monthly repayments

In the process, she also saves $2,381.68 for paying off her car earlier. And from now on, Mia has an extra $796.94 monthly to begin building a savings account much faster than she could have while paying off her debts. Just think about what has happened here for a moment. What difference could this make in your life, and that of your loved ones? How would you feel if you were debt-free? Imagine how quickly you can pay off your house if you added your car, credit card, and personal loan payments (because that money is freed now) to your mortgage. Or how about if you invested it intelligently?

As you can see, it is possible to pay off your debt sooner than banks and other financial institutions make it seem like. You must, however, take responsibility for your own finances, or someone else will. And if you hand over this responsibility, the results may not be as exciting as you would like them to be.

4

WHAT YOU SHOULD KNOW ABOUT CREDIT - THE GOOD, THE BAD AND THE UGLY

Credit has been available for hundreds of years. Today, credit can be used to buy a variety of items from clothing and food, to cars and houses. It is an excellent tool by itself when used responsibly. Credit, by definition, is getting value now and paying later, usually with interest added by the lender. The danger with credit comes when users fail to control their emotions and misuse it. There are several common ways to get credit, such as mortgages, car loans, personal loans, and credit card debt. Of these, credit card debt is one type that has become a problem for many people,

THE WORLD OF CREDIT CARDS

Credit cards came into use in the United States of America in the 1920s. They were meant to be paid off in full at the end of the money. The use of credit cards boomed in the 1950s. These days there are a variety of credit cards that involve rewards, membership, and fees. According to America's Debt Help Organization (n.d.), 70% of US adults own at least one credit card.

Credit cards offer benefits to both lenders and borrowers. We'll talk about their importance to consumers later in the chapter. For now, let's discuss how credit cards advantage lenders. Credit card issuers make billions of dollars every year from interest charges. They earn income when you make credit card purchases as they can keep up to 2% of the transaction value, according to America's Debt Help Organization. Also, lenders may charge fees such as late fees, insurance fees, card advances, administration fees, and annual membership charges. As you can see, there's every reason for lenders to try to attract consumers to apply and get credit.

How Credit Cards Work

All credit cards work the same way irrespective of type. During the first step, you apply for a credit card with a financial institution. But before you apply, it is vital to shop around for a cheaper credit with incentives you know you'll use. You can easily do your research online and choose the type of card that meets your needs. To ensure affordability, run online calculators that can help you determine if you'll be able to make the necessary payments or not.

Each credit card will have features such as credit limits and payment deadlines. Once your application is approved, your card issuer will send the card via mail or ask you to collect it at a local branch. Once you get the card, you need to activate it, and then you'll be ready to use it. But I must do my duty and inform you that as much as a credit card is a useful tool, it can also be a source of financial trouble. So, it is essential to apply for a credit card only when you have attained control over your spending habits. Otherwise, it is easy to quickly pile up massive debt and struggle to make the required payments and attract a lousy credit record.

Eight Common Types of Credit cards

There are several different kinds of credit cards available in the finance industry. All of them work on revolving debt, a type of loan with a set spending limit, which automatically renews immediately when you pay off the debt. With a credit card, you can carry a balance and repay the loan over time. Here are eight credit card types you are likely to find in the market.

- **Rewards cards**. Rewards cards offer attractive incentives such as immediate cashback or points that can be redeemed for free nights at some hotel chains, for example. They tend to have a mixture of annual fees and high-interest rates, and may also set a limit on the rewards. I remember three years ago; my card issuer frequently called me to ask if I knew of the rewards attached to my credit card. I had already realized that it would be easy to begin spending on things like lunches at luxury restaurants, even if I could cook myself, so I never activated the rewards.
- **Retail cards**. These kinds of cards have

become very common. They are of two types, open-loop (for use in other stores than the issuer) and closed-loop (to be used only in the issuing store). They usually have high-interest rates.

- **Traditional credit cards**. They are ordinary cards you use to charge purchases in various stores and gas stations. Most stores accept these cards.

- **Balance transfer cards**. Sometimes you may become overwhelmed by your credit card debt and not know what to do next. This is where balance transfer credit cards can be of a welcome aid. The reason is that you can get 0% interest on your balance over a given period of time such as 21 months, and 0% interest on purchases for the first six to 21 months (America's Debt Help Organization, n.d.). To use these cards, you may have to pay a transfer charge, annual fees, and also have a good credit score to qualify and be approved. This is essentially credit card refinancing.

- **Premium rewards cards**. Certain consumers have become good at paying their credit cards and tend to spend big. Such responsible cardholders can apply and get premium rewards credit cards. These cards have some of the best rewards, including cashback, travel insurance, free foreign transactions, and many other incentives. Just like rewards cards, there is a cost associated with owning premium reward cards.

- **Low-interest credit cards**. These cards are great to use to consolidate your debt and either pay a lower premium or pay off your liabilities quicker. The reason is that you get charged little interest. Unfortunately, not everybody qualifies to own these cards. They are usually given to consumers with good credit scores and above.

- **Secured credit cards**. The cards we have discussed above are usually unsecured or not backed up by collateral. Secured cards are backed up by assets such as a cash deposit to protect lenders in case you default on your payments or terms. Usually, these cards are used by people who have bad credit records as a tool to build a good credit history.

The Good about Credit Cards to Users

There are several advantages to credit cards if they're correctly used. Of course, the advantages may differ from one kind of a card to another. Let's discuss the following six benefits of owning a credit card.

- You can use a credit card to help boost your credit rating, especially if you have a poor credit record or limited credit history. However, your card issuer may charge you higher interest rates since they may deem you a high-risk borrower. The way to overcome these high-interest rates is to pay the outstanding amount in full each month. If you do this consistently, your credit card score will soon increase and lower your risk profile. And this means you'll be able to get future credit with favorable terms.

- You may get great rewards and extra benefits. A variety of cards come with different benefits and incentives. It is vital to choose the right benefits and rewards for you and not opt for incentives you would barely use. For example, if you travel often,

an airline credit card that offers mileage
points might be your best choice.

- Credit cards can help you cut down on debt.
  This advantage depends on the kind of card
  you use. The types that help you reduce your
  debt are the balance transfer and low-
  interest credit cards. With the balance
  transfer card, you can transfer your high-
  cost existing debt to a signed account and
  frequently at lower interest rates. At these
  low annual percentage rates (APR), it
  becomes possible to pay off debt if you pay
  more than the minimum monthly amount.

- Credit cards allow you to spread the
  payment of a larger item. In some cases, you
  may want to purchase an item such as a car,
  a phone, a smart television, and so on, but
  don't have ready cash to make a quick
  transaction, especially if it is a good deal. In
  some cases, you may want to make
  emergency car repairs or pay for medical
  bills. The possibilities are almost endless.
  That's when a credit card can assist you with
  spreading the cost of the item over a more
  extended period. What this does is reduce
  the impact on your income.

- Credit cards can be like getting interest-free loans. There are certain cards that don't charge any interest if you pay at an agreed time during a given period of owning the account. However, to qualify, you may need to have a good credit rating.
- You may qualify for purchase protection. In some countries, credit card holders may be eligible for protection on transactions they make with their cards. For example, in the UK, government policy allows you to claim back your money for a bad product or service on a credit card transaction of between £100 and £30,000.

What's Bad about Credit Cards

It is the nature of things that where there's good, bad is around the corner. Hence, the importance of becoming aware of both the good and the bad to place yourself advantageously as much as possible. While credit cards offer excellent advantages, they may also be problematic to users. Let's talk about the three main disadvantages of credit cards.

- **Most, if not all of them, attract fees**. The lender can charge legally-allowed fees of various kinds, especially if you don't repay as agreed in the contract. These fees can quickly add up into a substantial sum and could help trap you into a perpetual credit card debt. Of course, the best way to avoid expenses like these is to do as initially agreed when you signed your credit card contract. If you're not able to pay, get in touch with your issuer to make payment arrangements.

- **Limited use.** Some credit card issuers may restrict you from using your card in specific ways. For example, you may be allowed to use your gas card only at specified gas stations, while in some cases, you may attract charges if you withdraw cash unless it is included in the credit agreement.

- **Increased possibility of debt.** It is a wise move to only apply for a credit card once you have nipped your spending habits in the bud. The reason is that credit cards make it exceedingly easy to make compulsive purchases. If you know you're an impulsive buyer and currently have a credit card, better keep it as far away from you as possible. Also, if you happen to miss making agreed payments, it becomes easy for your debt to spiral out of your hands and for you to stay indebted because the often high-interest rates charged can quickly cause the balance to skyrocket. This is not a pleasant situation. I know the feeling.

As you can see, credit cards by themselves are not necessarily bad. It is the way the cardholder uses it that can turn out to be a problem. So, and I emphasize, ensure you're emotionally and mentally ready to manage your buying habits before you apply for a credit card.

How to Use a Credit Card to Build Your Credit Score

Credit scores are classified into five categories, from very poor to exceptional as follows:

- Very poor: 300 – 579. This score ranks below the ordinary US borrower's average rating, and lenders consider you a high risk to advance money.
- Fair: 580 – 669. Your score is still lower than that of a typical US consumer with debt, but

many lenders will approve such credit applicants.

- Good: 670 – 739. Your score is about the average for a US borrower. Lenders see you as a somewhat reliable borrower and are willing to lend you money.
- Very good: 740 – 799. Your score is above the average of a typical US credit user. Lenders consider you a great candidate to advance credit to you at respectable interest rates.
- Exceptional: 800 – 850. With this score, you are considered an exceptional borrower and lenders see you as highly reliable and may give you great interest rates.

These scores are based on the Fair Isaac Corporation (FICO) calculation model. Most of the top lenders use this model to make credit-lending decisions. This score is based on the information captured in your credit report that is provided by credit bureaus. Your credit score is calculated based on the following variables:

- Your payment history, which contributes 35% to your credit score.

- The amounts of credit you owe, and it contributes 30% to your overall score.
- The length of your credit history, which adds 15% to your total credit score.
- New credit you've applied for recently accounts for 10% of your credit score.
- The blend of your credit accounts adds the last 10% to complete your credit score.

The above variables provide a variety of gates through which to improve your credit score. As you can see, 80% of your FICO score comes from your payment history, the amounts you owe, and the length of your credit history. These are the areas to focus on.

Your payment history affects your credit history the most. What does this mean to you regarding your credit card debt? Simply that you should religiously pay your credit card on time. The best way to do this is to automate this process. This means that you link your credit card account with your checking account. Once that is done, you set the amount of money to transfer regularly on a given date. Ensure the date is about three to five days after your employer deposits your paycheck into your checking account. Also, ensure you pay at least the minimum amount as per your credit card statement. The bonus of handling your credit card payments in this way is that your card will stay open for a long time, and thus help build a good to exceptional credit score.

One factor that influences your credit score on credit cards is how much of the balance you're using. This is called the utilization ratio. The lower it is, the easier it is for you to pay off the full balance each month. This means that it is better to use only the credit card amount you know you'll be able to pay off at the end of each month. Your budget will come in handy to figure out this amount.

To lengthen the life of your credit history, keep your old credit cards open. As we said above, your credit score will get a needed boost. However, be careful that the cost of maintaining these credit cards open does not weigh you down financially. If it does, close the cards and focus on the other elements that affect your credit score.

After going through the above information, you may feel like a credit card is not a suitable tool for you and your circumstances. There are other ways you may wish to explore before applying for a credit card.

ALTERNATIVES TO USING CREDIT CARDS

You may be one of those people who feel that getting a credit card is a recipe for financial disaster. Credit cards are an excellent financial tool provided you use them responsibly. It's possible to be a responsible credit cardholder and still feel that the cost of maintaining one is too much for you. In any of the two reasons above, the best alternative is to consider borrowing money from your family or even friends. Loans by family or friends are big business. For example, it is estimated that loans from family and friends in the United States of America make up to $89 billion annually (America's Debt Help Organization, n.d.). I'm sure you'd agree that this money is huge. The good thing is that you can also join this market, but ensure you use these loans purely to help you handle emergencies while you're getting your finances sorted out.

The most important thing is to loan money from friends and family properly to avoid messing up personal relationships.

Borrowing from Family and Friends Responsibly

In the family and friends loan market, lenders tend to be flexible about payment arrangements. Unfortunately, some borrowers abuse this advantage. They forget that they're getting low-interest rates or even zero interest. The problem is that such borrowers can swiftly tarnish the relationship they have with their family or friend. How then do you avoid getting into such a fix?

The best way to protect the relationship while still getting financial help is to treat a family or friend loan as if you're borrowing from a financial institution such as a bank. In other words, it is necessary to draw up and sign a simple credit agreement. The basic elements to include in your loan agreement are:

- The amount of money you're borrowing. This is called the principle in finance jargon.
- The interest rate you'll be expected to pay if applicable. In most cases, your friends and family may not charge you any interest.
- The timing of your repayments and the amounts involved.
- Clauses that specify what the lender may do in case you default on your credit agreement. This essentially serves to protect the lender because the most prominent risk involved

for them is losing their money. This is standard practice in the credit market. The lender always adds protection clauses to try to prevent you from defaulting. But, you may also ensure you add provisions that protect you.

Note that your lender can take legal action against you if you default on the credit agreement. Hence, there's a possibility your personal assets could be attached to recoup the loan. Something worse can actually happen if you default. The personal relationship you have with your lender may fall apart and can become especially tough to repair it. The good thing is that you can help prevent tarnishing the relationship by keeping wide lines of communication with your lender. Even when you realize you may not be able to meet the payment deadline, ensure you stay in touch with your lender. They will probably understand your situation and be open to an adjustment of some sort.

Most importantly, ensure that you don't do verbal agreements. They work but are not sufficient, especially if legal actions get involved. It is always better to have a written contract and have it signed by all parties. The beauty of a written contract is that it helps capture all the pertinent details of the credit agreement and can protect you during a potential legal battle.

5

TRACK YOUR SPENDING AND ELIMINATE UNNECESSARY EXPENSES

K ristin, a writer, like many initially ignored money advice suggesting that she should track her spending. She just could not see the point of doing what she thought was a simple thing. In her mind, she always believed that she had a good grasp of her expenses. This is understandable considering that this wordsmith isn't a shopaholic who can't walk past a J.Crew without stopping by and buying. She felt she knew enough about her day-to-day expenses.

One day she decided to go over her transaction history to see how much she had spent on different categories over time. She got a shock when she found out that she had spent a whole $636 on Amazon with only a pair of hiking boots, and some shoes to show for it. This savvy writer admitted that the purchases she made on Amazon weren't necessarily bad but that she had underestimated how quickly they quickly added up to a substantial sum. This ignited a thought in her mind that made her doubtful that she was good with her money. The money that she had spent on Amazon after she thought a little about it was enough to cover weeks of groceries, or even part of her month's rent, and so on.

Finally, Kristin decided to take the advice of tracking her expenses or at least give this important money habit a trial. She discovered that the exercise was quite simple, but it packed real power. Within a few weeks, she began to have a feel of how she spent her hard-earned money. Best of all, she started to see where she could cut her expenses so that she could put away extra cash in a savings account. She learned a crucial lesson, and she now knows that having financial problems, and the stress that comes with them, is something that is avoidable.

As you read Kristin's story above, you may have picked up a few reasons why tracking your expenses is a vital part of your money management activities.

There are many more reasons for tracking your expenses.

TWELVE REASONS WHY IT'S IMPORTANT TO TRACK YOUR EXPENSES

1. Tracking your expenses helps you stay focused on the health of your financial situation.
2. When you regularly track your expenses, it soon becomes clear to you whether you are making progress towards your financial goals or not.
3. Control is an important aspect of money management, and when you track your finances, you'll notice an improvement in handling them. As you record your transactions, you are forced to question the importance of each of your buying decisions, and this sets you up for easier and astute future purchasing.
4. It is one of the rules of management that you cannot manage what you don't measure. Tracking your expenses helps you stay on

budget and avoid making unnecessary expenses.

5. Some of us tend to forget that our finances are our individual responsibilities. Tracking expenses reconnects you to this responsibility and keeps you accountable for your future financial goals.

6. One major weakness some of us have is lack of self-discipline. You'll notice that when you track your expenses regularly, your level of discipline will improve, and subsequently, you'll experience less financial stress.

7. It improves your financial security.

8. As you regularly monitor your transactions, you'll discover ways you may have overlooked for saving more money. For example, you may realize that some online subscriptions you have are simply wasteful because you barely use them.

9. The habit of tracking your expenses will help you reduce impulse buying because it will force you to consult your budget or think things through before purchasing goods or services.

10. Debt is one of the things that pull us away from enjoying financial independence.

When you track your expenses, you'll find that you begin to avoid unnecessary debt. In fact, this habit of monitoring expenses is a great motivation tool to steer away from transactions that may involve getting into debt.

11. Monitoring expenses helps you reach your financial objectives by aiding you to spend on items that match your priorities.

12. Last but not least, when you track your expenses, you get your finances organized and prevent financial problems.

As you can see, there are a variety of good reasons to monitor how you use your money. It is particularly helpful to keep track of your expenses if you are a spender. You are probably wondering how this is done.

HOW TO KEEP TRACK OF YOUR EXPENSES

If you have been working on altering your habits as suggested in Chapter 2, you'll find it easier to do what I'll show you in a moment. To be able to win your battle with money, you certainly must change your behavior regarding money. The first important action to implement regularly is to create a budget. This is a plan upon which to guide your spending and to ensure you don't spend money that you don't have. In other words, you create a spending plan before making any purchases.

When I was in the corporate world, we had a company-wide schedule geared towards budgeting the organization's spending. The plan covered all kinds of items from nuts, bolts, personal protective equipment, entertainment, training, and so on.

Now, I want you to think of yourself as a business. If you were the manager of your business, would you run it without a budget? Of course not. In fact, if you ever applied for business finance, you know the financier required you to have a cash flow forecast as one of the requirements. The game of money is intellectual, not emotional, as many of us erroneously make it to be. So, begin by embracing budgeting your money. Let me deal with some common objections people give to avoid creating home budgets before we talk about the budgeting process itself.

Common Objections to Regular Budgeting

Some people give various reasons for not budgeting.

Unfortunately, not doing this vital financial management step sets you up for a cycle of money problems. The kinds of budgeting objections or excuses some people give shouldn't block you from cash flow planning. Here are a few of those objections:

- **I don't believe a budget will work for me.** The reality is that the reason a budget may not work is that it is just a tool like a spade. It is the user who makes it work. It is not as restrictive as some think. What it helps you do is avoid impulsive buying. If you have an item that you believe you should buy, simply include it in the budget. However, remember that your money is limited, so you cannot buy everything you want at the same time.

- **I don't have enough money to budget.** It is not so much about the amount of money as it is about planning what you spend your income on. In fact, learning to budget while your income is low prepares you well to handle large sums when the time comes. Remember that the way you do small things is the way you do big things.

- **Budgeting takes too long.** You are either in control or not when it comes to your finances. And you cannot be in control without first budgeting your expenses. So, whether it takes a long or short time shouldn't be the main issue. At any rate, there are tools that can help you budget quicker than in the old days of doing many things manually. Furthermore, remember that when you begin to do something new, you tend to be slow at the start, but you'll improve your speed as you progress.

- **Fear of discovering the reality of how you spend money.** Budgeting involves tracking your expenses. Some people are afraid of facing facts about their spending. They are in denial. That's why most don't even voice this objection directly. The reality is that unless you face the facts, you don't deserve to reap the benefits of sound financial management.

If you had any one of the above objections or any other tiresome excuse, realize that your financial future rests squarely on your shoulders. You must take ownership and drive it to where you want.

How to Budget Your Expenses

Budgeting your expenses is a process that follows a specific sequence. That's why it is sometimes called cash flow planning. You can't spend cash before you earn it, or you shouldn't. I'm taking it you have an income, preferably regular such as monthly or even weekly. Here's how to go about the budgeting process.

- The best place to begin is to discover what your current expenditures are. Your account statements provide that kind of information. So, take inventory of all your accounts, such as credit cards, checking accounts, and so on.
- Categorize your expenses: start by manually grouping your expenses into categories such as communications, groceries, subscription services, etc. Some bank accounts actually automatically tag your purchases and allocate them into different categories. This may also help you see where you are bleeding a lot of your money.
- Choose a budgeting tool that's easy for you to use. There are several tools you can use to create your budget. Here are three that you may like:
- Use a budgeting app – There are many

applications you can use, such as "You Need a Budget," "Mint," and "Clarity Money" which are designed for easy money management. These tools work on zero-based budgeting. This means that all your income is allocated for spending on various items, including savings and debt. They can also help you allocate a certain amount of spendable income every month, depending on what you're taking in and paying out. With "You Need a Budget" you can sync with your bank account, set financial goals, and even customize your spending categories. Access to resources like budgeting advice and free money workshops are also available on this app.

- Spreadsheet-based budgeting – The beauty of spreadsheets is that they are easy to customize and can be set up to create reports that help you see your expenses at a glance. This is a wonderful tool if you're not a fan of apps.

- The envelope method – The envelope method is cash-based or even credit card-based, and works when personally making transactions. You begin by identifying all the categories or items you can pay cash for. Then, you allocate a real live envelope for each of the categories or items you identified. Finally, once you receive your income, simply deposit the budgeted money into each of your envelopes. This is the amount you are willing to spend on the items and no more. When you go shopping for groceries, take the appropriate envelope with you to the stores, with no excess cash, and when the money runs out, you stop buying. This is one powerful way to develop self-discipline.

Record your expenses. Note down all your transactions immediately after you make them. If it's not possible to record them immediately, do so within a day or two. If you have a spouse, share this financial planning process with them and agree on the steps you'll take to support your goals. Each partner should record all the purchases they make, and all the transactions should be entered into your budgeting tool.

An important point to note here is that your budget may not work to a tee in the beginning. It will probably require tweaking and adjusting to make it work for you. If budgeting and tracking expenses are new to you, it is essential to keep reminding yourself why you're doing it in the first place.

You are now ready to begin the process of cleaning up your finances and reducing the stress that comes with money problems. But this by itself isn't enough. There is more you can still do to improve your financial health.

HOW TO ELIMINATE UNNECESSARY PURCHASES

One of the more challenging prospects of personal finance is determining the best way to use your money. You have already begun the process by learning how to create a budget, but it doesn't stop here. You still must stick to the budget, and this is where self-control can be your savior. Let's go over some ways you can eliminate unnecessary spending:

Create a grocery list before going to the stores

A few days ago, I wrote down a list to buy a few things we needed at home. Strangely, I still purchased some items that were not on my list because I felt that they were necessary. When you enter the store, your psychology generally changes.

The interior of the stores is mostly designed to alter the way you feel while you're there. There are so many cues to trigger certain behaviors you may have been programmed to exhibit earlier in your life. For example, some stores have bakeries at the back, and the smell of freshly-baked bread can activate your emotions, which can cause you to buy bread even if you had not planned to. The way to solve this problem is to draw up a detailed list of the items you want to buy. Immediately as you enter the store, take out the list and go straight to the aisle where the items you seek are displayed. Do this until you have thrown each of the items on your list into a cart. When you have a grocery list, you minimize the chances of temptation and compulsive buying. A bonus is that when you prepare the list beforehand, there's little chance of forgetting essential items to buy, and thus saving time and money on gasoline.

Avoid carrying debit or credit cards, or excess cash with you.

It's strange but a reality that we find it easy to whip out a credit card and buy things that were not in our plans. The biggest trigger to such impulsive buying is the millions and millions of cues around us. As we discussed in Chapter 2, signals initiate routines that are linked to specific rewards. And we are wired to keep looking for signs that can lead to rewards. Unfortunately, we are not always conscious of these under the radar processes. Have you ever heard of Parkinson's Law? This law, as applied to money, says that your expenses will grow to consume all the available funds. So, to avoid spending money unnecessarily, consider having with you only the money that is allocated for a specific purpose.

Cook your meals at home

I know it is tough to regularly cook your own meals after a long day at work. Have you ever tracked how expensive it is to eat out compared to eating home-cooked meals? A 2018 study by Wellio, a home-cooked meal planning online service, revealed astounding insights. In the study, the researchers analyzed 86 popular recipes and found that it is about five times more expensive to order restaurant meals than it is to cook the same dish at home. What about using meal kits? Well, a meal kit was found to be three times as expensive as cooking the same recipe at home. Protein-based restaurant meals were found to be the most expensive when ordered from a restaurant.

The way to save on eating out is to cook at home. If

you are short on time, one option to consider is cooking on a Sunday and freeze your meals for use during the week. At first, you may start by cooking meals to eat two or three times during the week. Over time you can increase this to five days a week or even add another cooking day during the week.

Cancel club memberships or entertainment bills

It tends to be easy to forget about your automatically recurring monthly bills, such as gym subscriptions. One time I subscribed to a satellite television that had over 500 channels, and I mainly used the sports channels. Eventually, I asked myself what the point was. So, I reduced my subscriptions to a cheaper one. This is not unique to satellite subscriptions. There are many people who buy recurring gym memberships and barely use them. I know because I once bought one when I was recuperating from a knee injury but did not use it after returning to work. However, I still had to pay monthly because I had signed up for a 12-month membership. If you have such subscriptions, cancel them, and you'll see what impact this can have on your budget. As a matter of fact, you can use this extra cash to pay off your debt quicker than you ever thought possible, as shown in Chapter 3.

Put any bonuses into your savings account.

Most of us become new people immediately when we receive bonuses from our jobs. We tend to become compulsive buyers instantly. Instead of quickly spending your bonus, what about putting it in your savings account? Doing so will give you time to think about better uses for your bonus. However, if you have a plan that helps you get ahead financially, like paying off your debt, you may go ahead and use the bonus for that purpose only.

Remove your card details from online shopping accounts.

Most devices give you the option to store your card details when shopping online. This makes it easy for you to make future purchases. When you make your first online purchase, you'll notice that the process is lengthy because it requires necessary details like shipping address, email address, debit or credit card details, and so on. But on your subsequent purchases, the process is fast and easy. This can suddenly suck you in and encourage impulsive buying: that's why removing your card details on online shopping sites can be a great move to stop making unnecessary purchases.

Other ways

- Try buying groceries online. This works particularly well if the sights and smells in grocery stores easily influence you. You'll find that you are much more disciplined and able to stick to your budget.
- Pack and take lunch to work. It is easy to be tempted to buy meals like sandwiches that are usually strategically placed to trigger a buying response from you. But when you know you have lunch with you, this may not work as well, preventing an unnecessary purchase.
- If you drive your car to work, consider carpooling or even taking public transport. It goes without saying that doing this will reduce your fuel costs.
- Consider doing DIY projects. I know a friend of mine who bought a small beat-up Ford truck. He took it to a service mechanic for its first minor service and carefully observed as the mechanic changed the plugs, oil, and air filters. Since then, he's been doing the minor service himself. You can do the

same and also consider doing your own painting, landscaping, and so on.

There are more other ways for you to cut unnecessary expenses. The list I've provided should set you on the right track. Remember to keep your financial goal in mind on a daily basis so that you remain motivated to follow through on the ideas suggested throughout this book. If you feel that you are someone who struggles to maintain motivation when striving to achieve long-term goals, click here to download my *7 Essential Tips to Stay Motivated*, completely free. The full URL to this free bonus is located at the beginning of the book, after the copyright page.

6

HOW TO REDUCE THE COST OF YOUR NECESSARY SPENDING

When you are living from paycheck to paycheck, it's hard even to think you can save money. All you tend to see are massive obstacles blocking you from even the thought of saving. However, it is possible if you are determined, like this British teacher named Kathy Kelly.

According to *This is Money* (2008), Kathy lived on about £1 a day for a full year. Sounds impossible, doesn't it? Before you write this story off, listen to what happened, and perhaps you can pick up a few ideas to implement in your life right now. Kathy earned enough money, but like many, she wasted it on small things she didn't really need, such as eating out, takeout coffees, and so on. She filled her wardrobe with clothes she barely wore, and her fridge was packed with food items she hardly ate. Often, she dug into her overdraft facility.

Two things happened that inspired her to change her ways of using money. First, she saw a television program featuring a woman called Judith Levine, who explained how she lived on bare necessities for a year. The second thing was that Kathy's brother was getting married in a year's time. She decided she was going to save to buy her brother a wedding gift. The goal she set for herself was tough: she'd live on an average of £1 a day. How did she do it?

She began by stopping doing plenty of things she had become accustomed to. For example, she stopped reading glossy magazines, drinking Starbucks coffee, and eating Wagamama twice a week. That was not all. She went on to stop buying expensive clothes, shoes, and handbags at Bristol's upmarket stores. She replaced this habit by visiting discount stores and discount shelves to buy cheaper food.

Soon her skirt button wouldn't fasten: that's when she realized how tough it was to eat healthily on such a small budget. But she did not let this deter her from her goal. Instead, she became exceedingly knowledgeable at making perishable food items last longer. For example, she discovered that by placing red cabbages in the dark, they took longer to spoil. This lady had to be creative to keep her stomach full. She started to visit stores often for tasters. During the warmer months, she often picked berries and other fruits in the countryside.

She faced many challenges, for example, her friends couldn't understand her ways anymore, although some were supportive. But she also overcame many of them. For example, to entertain herself, she cut coupons from old magazines to attend events. As for transport, she got into the habit of hitch-hiking. All these challenges led her to realize, as she neared her goal, how much she had been wasting on food that at times she even threw away, on books she never read, and on coffees she bought just because she had nothing to do. Most importantly, she discovered that she knew very little about herself and that she wasn't as independent as she thought.

Why am I telling you this story? First, to simply impress upon your mind that if you genuinely want to hit your financial goal, you can certainly do it. Secondly, to bring to your awareness the fact that you can simply say something cannot be done until you have tried it and found it impossible to ace it.

Now, let me share with you several ideas that can help you cut your expenses on items that you *cannot* live without.

1. How to cut down on food costs

There are several ways to reduce your expenses on necessary food items. Here are five of the most important to seriously consider:

- **Shop at a discount store.** I'm sure you noticed as you read Kathy's story that she did this. If you tend to buy your food at pricey stores, know that you can still buy exactly the same kind of food items at lower prices if you switch stores.
- **Purchase store-brand products.** The kind of food that differs little between store-brand and name-brand includes staple items such as sugar, salt, flour, coffee, and many other products. The main difference lies in the packaging, not the contents. One helpful way of checking the similarities between the store-brand and name brand items is to compare the ingredients.
- **Grow your own vegetables.** There are several vegetable products you can easily

grow on your own. For example, you can plant your own spinach, tomatoes, green beans, red peppers, and so on in your backyard. The plus side is that your produce is unlikely to be full of pesticides that may be health hazards.

- **Buy bulk non-perishable items.** When you buy in bulk, usually, the cost per unit is lower than when buying individual items. This means that bulk buying saves you money. This idea works particularly well when you buy soap, sugar, salt, shampoo, and other non-perishable items.

- **Cook your meals at home.** We have already shown in Chapter 4 that home-cooked meals are cheaper than restaurant-delivered food. The plus for cooking at home is that you are absolutely sure of all the ingredients that go into making your dishes. Recently, I saw a social media post by someone asking for help with paying her debt quickly. Somebody asked her to share her monthly budget. When she shared her monthly spending plan, I discovered that she spent $300 on eating out. That was just over 10% of her gross income per month. If you're starved for ideas, recipe eBooks are available for as low as $0.99 on the Kindle Store.

2. Reduce insurance bills

There are several kinds of insurance products that most people have, such as a car, health, and homeowners. There are numerous opportunities to reduce the premiums you may currently be paying. Here are four ways you could use to get lower rates.

- **Downgrade your health plan.** This option may be right for you if you don't make frequent visits to your doctor's office. Obviously, you know your health and that of your family better than I do and can make an informed choice. The kind of health insurance you could downgrade to is the deductible plan, which covers you for emergencies. It's essential to check the details of your targeted health plan to ensure you can afford the out-of-pocket expenses.
- **Shop around for lower homeowners or rental insurance.** As the age of your credit history grows, your credit score may increase if you are a good payer. This behavior may result in better homeowners'

insurance. The starting point is to get multiple quotations and use them to request lower rates from your current insurer. Your insurer may accept your request because they don't usually like to lose customers to their competitors.

- **Bundle your homeowners and auto insurance.** This option may save you money if you insure your car and home with the same insurer. The reason for this is that you may get a good deal because of what you may consider a 'bulk' purchase. Further, doing this helps you manage your insurance efficiently as you'll be dealing with one insurer instead of two.

- **Switch from whole life insurance to term life insurance.** Term life insurance covers a member for a given period of time called a term. This means the insurer will pay if a member dies during the agreed-upon term. Term life insurance is cheaper per year compared to whole life insurance, and you may renew it after the term expires or convert to whole life insurance.

3. Save on your current debt.

We have covered how you can do this using car financing and auto insurance in Chapter 4. In effect, I showed you how to refinance your car at a lower interest rate with the same financier. But you can also refinance with a different financial institution. Make sure that it makes economic sense to move your balance over to another financier.

There are other ways available for you which you can take advantage of. Here we'll cover two of those opportunities.

- **Consider refinancing your home.** If your credit rating has improved since taking out your mortgage, this may be the best time to refinance. The reason is that your improved credit score may result in lower interest rates. This means if you refinance, you'll likely pay smaller monthly installments; then you can use the surplus money to increase your minimum monthly payment, and thus settle your debt much quicker. Refinancing with the same financial institution should be easy, but if you want to transfer your balance to another company, ensure it makes financial sense. In other words, check what the math says before moving over to your new financier.

- **Host a garage sale for items you don't use anymore.** Many of us have items such as clothing, gym equipment, bicycles, old computers, sports equipment, and so on that we may no longer be using. What's the point of keeping these things if we aren't using them? Simply clean them up and put them up for sale on eBay or Craigslist. Use the money you generate to pay your debt, either credit cards, personal loan, or mortgage. Remember not to overlook small sums of money.

4. Reduce energy bills

There are several overlooked ways to reduce your electricity bill. Unfortunately, most of us are so used to paying too much without even realizing how harmful this behavior is to us in the long-term. Let's go over some ways you could minimize your expenses on electricity.

- **Use a programmable thermostat.** A programmable thermostat is a device you can use to automatically adjust your cooling and heating to pre-set temperatures at scheduled time intervals. According to Lennox Industries (n.d.), installing and using a programmable thermostat to adjust your temperatures up or down by seven to ten degrees could save you about 10% on your annual heating and cooling costs.

- **Use power strips and timers.** Power strips are devices that are used to expand the wall socket to two or more outlets and sometimes include switches to individual appliances. As a result, you can use power strips to turn certain electrical appliances on and off as you wish. There are also 'smart' power strips that help manage electricity flow based on a given device called a control appliance. Timers automatically cut electricity to a power strip or electrical appliance either on or off at a given time of the day or night. This functionality, therefore, provides a convenient way to save on electricity bills.

- **Consider unplugging idling electrical and electronic devices.** When an electronic device is connected to a wall socket, it draws small amounts of power. If you have many devices, the total electricity that they draw can quickly increase your electricity bill. So it is with idling electrical appliances.

- **Drop the temperature of your water heater.** Many people heat their water to unnecessarily high temperatures. Such water loses high amounts of heat to the surroundings and wastes energy. The way to reduce these heat losses is to drop the temperature of your water heater. Yuko and Miller (2019) suggest that the appropriate temperature to set your water heater is 120 degrees Fahrenheit. This is good for two reasons. One is that you save energy and electricity costs, and secondly, such water is unlikely to scald anyone as it comes out of the tap. Two more ideas to consider are covering your heater and exposed hot water pipes with an insulating blanket. This material prevents your hot water from losing excessive heat to the surroundings and thus saves electricity.
- **Consider air sealing your home.** When you seal your home, you reduce the amount of air that enters or leaves it. When it's cold, if your home is not air sealed, cool air will enter the house and trigger your heater to

run for an unusually long time, increasing your energy bill. During warm outside weather, air from your home exits to the surroundings. Thus, your house rarely will reach your target temperature and cause your cooling system to run for longer. As a result, you will pay a higher electricity bill.

- **Switch to a cheaper energy plan.** Shop around for better deals when you're about to renew your fixed energy plan. Also, decide whether you want a combination of gas and electricity or either one of the two. Of course, your decision will depend on consumption and your region.

- **Install compact fluorescent lights (CFL) or light-emitting diode (LED) light bulbs.** CFL lamps are energy lamps that were designed to replace the traditional incandescent light bulbs. They are four times as energy-efficient as the old incandescent lights and last longer (Hamm, 2020). LED light bulbs are about 90% efficient than incandescent lamps (Energy Star, n.d.). The heat generated is absorbed into a built-in heat sink.

5. Reduce transport costs

The value of cars generally depreciates with time and can become expensive to maintain as they age. According to AAA Newsroom (n.d.), in 2015, the average annual cost to own and run an average sedan was $8,698. Of this amount, 42% was depreciation, 19.3% was fuel, and 12.8% was car insurance. Think about it. More than a third of the cost of owning a car is due to the loss of value of the automobile. Isn't this by itself enough to suggest the importance of reducing the cost of your transportation? It certainly is. So, let's go over ideas that could help in this regard.

- Use public transport more often or exclusively. When you use public transport, you immediately save on gas, parking, and the maintenance of your car. If using public transportation is an issue for you, consider sharing a ride to work with someone to reduce wear and tear on your vehicle, and gas consumption. In some countries, there are carpooling lanes, specially dedicated to helping you get to work easier and faster. Another option may be to stop using your car entirely and use rideshare services, especially if you live in major services.

- **Sell your car outright.** If you barely use your car, there's no point in keeping it. Instead, sell it and save on insurance, license fees, and maintenance. You can use the money you save to pay off your debt quicker.

6. Minimize entertainment expenses

Entertainment is one area that is relatively easy to overspend on. Here are some methods you could use to cut expenses in this area.

- **Reduce the time you spend watching television.** This is one of the most overlooked ways to cut costs. When you watch TV less, it becomes easy to downgrade your cable subscription from premium to basic. Why would you spend a fortune on premium cable and not get the benefit? It wouldn't make sense. Most importantly, you'll be exposed to fewer advertisements, which over time, can influence your buying decisions and encourage you to purchase things you may not need.
- **Cancel subscriptions to newspapers and**

magazines. If you don't have time to read the newspapers or magazines you have subscribed to, simply cancel them when renewal time comes. If you find you sometimes want to read these papers and magazines, simply go to your library.

WHAT TO DO WITH YOUR SURPLUS MONEY

The intention of the past five chapters (Chapter 2 to Chapter 6) was to provide you with information and action steps you should take to have surplus money after expenses. At this point, you know the importance of budgeting and sticking to it. In fact, you have resolved to make cash flow planning a routine part of your financial life. If you've done what we suggested above, you now have a surplus, and it's time to learn how to save so that you can materialize the goal you set in Chapter 1. The most appropriate tool you'll be using is a savings account.

WHAT IS A SAVINGS ACCOUNT?

Some people confuse between saving and investing. Right off the bat, I'd like to clarify how the two are similar and different. Saving money simply means putting cash away to access it on short notice without penalties or fees. Like investing, saving is done to achieve a specific purpose and usually in the short term. The most significant difference between saving and investing is the risk of losing your money. Savings are less riskier but typically attract lower returns than investing.

On the other hand, investing is the process of putting money into the right investment vehicle to get as high a return as possible. In other words, investing serves to grow your wealth. With investing, you vie for a long-term goal: to achieve a given objective in 10 years or more.

A savings account is a bank account where you deposit your money. It is even possible to get a savings account for free, especially if it is an online savings account. Let's now go ahead and talk about the details of savings and savings accounts. When you save your hard-earned cash in a savings account, you get a few advantages. The first most important benefit is safety. It is far safer to stash your cash in a savings account than under your mattress or piggy bank because it can be easily stolen or lost due to fire. In the US, the risk of losing your money in a savings account is mitigated if you save with a bank or financial institution insured with the Federal Deposit Insurance Corporation (FDIC). The FDIC covers you for up to $250,000 per insured bank. According to the FDIC (n.d.), "Since 1933, no depositor has lost a penny of FDIC-insured funds." The US is not the only country with this kind of a safety net for your saved funds. In the UK, the Financial Services Compensation Scheme (FSCS) protects your savings for up to £85,000 per insured financial institution.

There are other advantages to putting money in a savings account.

- Your money can earn interest and grow. This means a savings account can actually help you achieve your financial goal faster than having the money sitting at home. The interest you get is called compound interest. With this interest, you gain interest in your deposited money and the interest you've earned. So, your money can snowball depending on the balance. For example, if you deposit just $50 a month into a savings account that pays 1.50% interest per year and compounds monthly, at the end of five years, you'll get $3,116.42. Interest rates depend on the state of the economy and how competitive your bank is.

- The most notable advantage for many people is that it is not easy to spend the saved money since you cannot easily access it as easily as when it's in your wallet.
- It helps you avoid taking unnecessary debt; therefore, it can help you reach your financial goals faster.

The major disadvantage of typical savings accounts is that the interest you get may be lower than inflation. Thus, your money may actually lose its buying power as the years progress. But there's a way to mitigate this problem, and we will talk about it later in this chapter. If you remember that the purpose of saving is to keep your money safe, then this should not deter you from opening a savings account. One thing is for sure; a savings account is genuinely better than a checking account, which is mainly a transactional account. Note, however, that in the US, the Federal Reserve has placed a limit on the number of withdrawals and transfers on your savings account. If you think about it, this makes sense. If you withdraw often, what's the point of having a savings account at all? You'd be good to open and use a checking account, instead.

After the work you did on your finances, you should be in a position to know how much money you'll be able to save without living like a pauper. What's the next step to take?

SHOP AROUND FOR A SUITABLE TYPE OF SAVINGS ACCOUNT

There are a variety of savings accounts in the financial industry. These accounts may differ from one country to the next. But the principle to follow is to choose a savings account that allows you to meet your needs.

1. Basic Savings Accounts

Basic savings accounts are ordinary accounts you use to hold your money in. You earn interest and can also withdraw your money based on the restrictions set by the Federal Reserve or the institution running financial affairs in your country. You are, however, allowed to deposit money into the account as often as you wish. A basic savings account is right for you if you have simple needs.

2. Online Savings Accounts

Online savings accounts are popular in the technological world we live in. These accounts allow financial institutions to run on lower overheads than traditional banks, and therefore, offer higher interest rates. In addition, online savings accounts have little to no monthly fees, and thus, can help you grow your money faster than basic savings accounts. In most cases, there's no set minimum balance required to keep your account active. But some accounts cap the maximum balance. If you are tech-savvy, online savings are definitely a good fit. You can do many banking activities online, including depositing cash from a variety of sources and doing transfers. To open this kind of account, you'll need to have a linked account (such as a checking account). Some online banks with no brick-and-mortar branches have online checking accounts you can use to write checks, make purchases and cash withdrawals using debit cards, and even pay a variety of bills online.

3. Student Savings Accounts

When you mainly have low balances in your basic savings account, the fees may quickly wipe out your money. So, it does make financial sense to use a traditional savings account. This is a situation common among students. Hence, some financial institutions offer student savings accounts that have no monthly fees. It is wise to read the terms of the student savings account because, at some point, as you age, your account converts into a basic type and begins to attract maintenance fees.

4. Goal-Focused Savings Accounts

Do you have a specific savings goal in mind, such as buying a big wedding gift for your sister or brother? Great. There are banks that can help you open a savings account just for the purpose of assisting you in achieving your goal. These accounts are called goal-oriented savings accounts. They are designed to help you stay motivated to go after and hit your target. However, the interests you get do not differ from those of traditional savings accounts.

5. Notice Savings Accounts

You can find savings accounts called notice deposits in some countries such as the UK and South Africa. The reason behind the name is because you need to give advance notice to withdraw your money. Typical notice periods start from 30 days. The interest rates added to your balance don't differ much from those of traditional savings accounts. The advantage is that with these kinds of accounts, you avoid the temptation to make unnecessary withdrawals, improving your chances of achieving your savings goals. If you know you won't need immediate access to your cash, an account like this is suitable for you.

Now you know what kinds of savings accounts are available and I'm sure as you were reading, you made a choice about the type that suits you. What's the next stage of your process to build a good cash reserve? You should now find out the ideal financial institution to open a savings account with.

WHERE TO OPEN YOUR SAVINGS ACCOUNT

Different people have different financial needs. So, there is no single savings account and financial institution that will cater to all people's needs. However, in choosing a financial institution, it is imperative to ensure that your money is safe first, and then, to ensure that your money will work as hard as possible. Importantly, make sure you're charged the lowest fees possible to maximize your returns.

There are many banks to choose from, whether you're in the UK or the US, but if you want a high yield savings account, the best savings account to open is an online savings kind. It attracts higher interest rates, and you get charged lower fees or no fees at all. Select an FDIC-insured financial institution if you're in the US or FSCS-insured if you're in the UK. There are also online services that help you choose the right online savings account. In the US, you may use www.bankrate.com, while in the UK one of the best services you can employ is www.-moneysupermarket.com.

Now, allow me to list and discuss the top three US banks that provide good online savings accounts, as suggested by Bankrate (May 2020). This is important: when you research these online savings accounts, the rates I mention here may have changed.

- **Live Oak Bank:** This bank was founded in 2008 to fund veterinary practices and is FDIC-insured. Currently, the bank supports businesses in other industries. The annual percentage yield (APY) or yearly interest rate you can get is 1.55% on any minimum balance, compounded on a daily basis. When you open an online saving account with Live Oak Bank, you'll have access to online account management. You can manage your account on the bank's mobile app. However, you won't have access to a branch. Best of all, you pay no monthly account fees and can make up to six withdrawals per month.

- **Capital One**: This bank offers you zero monthly fees and no minimum balance on your savings account. You can earn 1.50% interest per annum and make up to six withdrawals per month. Not only does this bank have local branches, but it is also FDIC-insured. Also, you can make automatic transfers and deposits by using the digital tools available.

- **Sallie Mae**: This bank makes its mark by offering private student loans, but it also provides savings accounts. Its online savings account gives you a 1.35% interest per annum, compounded daily, and paid monthly. You don't need to have a minimum balance to get this interest rate, and importantly, your account attracts no monthly fees. With this online account, you may transfer between internal and external bank accounts. Note that when you transfer between the internal and external accounts, it may take up to five days for the funds to clear.

Let's now look at the top three online savings accounts in the UK, as provided by **www.moneysupermarket.com**. The accounts discussed here can be opened with a small amount of money. Note that at the time you research these accounts, the rates I mention may have changed.

- **Yorkshire Building Society**: The name of the online savings account with reasonable interest is called Internet Safer Plus Issue 3. You can get between 0.2% and 1.02% annual effective rate (AER) that is variable (that is, not fixed). The interest you get is dependent upon the balance you have. The higher your balance, the higher the AER you get. The minimum balance to maintain this account is £1, and you have access to online account management to check your balances, interest, and make online transactions. Once you open this account, you'll be able to access funds for withdrawal after 14 days. The good thing is that with this account, you can make unlimited withdrawals. This financial institution is FSCS-insured for your safety.

- **Paragon Bank**: The online savings account you may want to consider is called the Easy Access Savings Account. It starts from a minimum of £1 and caps at a maximum of £500,000. The variable annual interest you get on your balance is 0.50%, and the growth is calculated daily but paid monthly or annually. Your savings are secure with Paragon Bank as it is FSCS-insured, while you are allowed to make unlimited withdrawals and deposits.

- **Automobile Association (AA)**: This FSCS-insured banking institution was initially founded in 1905 to protect motorists. It now has over 15 million members (AA, n.d.). Its online savings offering gives you a 0.75% annual interest for the first 12 months. After that, the interest drops to 0.10% after the removal of the 0.75% first 12 months bonus.

Unlike the two accounts we've covered above, this one requires a minimum balance of £100 and a top limit of £2,000,000. With this account, you can save your money regularly or deposit lump sums, and the interest is calculated daily and paid on the annual anniversary of your account.

Now you have selected the financial institution to open an online, or any other savings account with. It's time to visit the bank with the required documentation and open the account. Ensure you confirm that the main terms and conditions of the account are as you found in your research. If something doesn't make sense to you, ask immediately and before you sign on the dotted line. A good customer service bank employee should be able to help you. You are now ready to automate your saving, so you don't mistakenly miss any month.

HOW TO SET UP EFFORTLESS SAVING IN YOUR SAVINGS ACCOUNT

We have now made serious progress on our way to help you save for your financial goals. This is now the time to make the savings. You've opened the savings account you believe will meet your needs and with a financial institution that is safe to bank at. How would you feel if you could automatically save the amount of money you want regularly and not worry about overspending and not stash something away? There is a way, and I'll show you how to do it right now.

I'm going to assume you get paid once every month for this exercise and that you already have a checking account for daily transactions and depositing your paycheck. If you don't have a checking account, I suggest you open one, especially if you make frequent transactions. The first thing I want you to do is to create a table with the following headings: account name, bank name, and account type. Under the account name column, write the name of each of your bank accounts. In the second column, add the name of the bank corresponding with each of your accounts. In the last column, add the type of account for each of the account names from the first column. Your table may look something like this (I've used fictitious names for illustration purposes):

Account Name	Bank	Account Type
Daily Transactions	Trust Bank	Checking account
Emergency Fund	Alive Capital	Online savings account
Credit Builder	Bill Building Society	Credit card

Now, log in to your checking account and link it to your savings account. In my example above, I would log in to the Daily Transaction account I have with Trust Bank. Then, I'd navigate to the necessary menu options to link it with the Emergency Fund (my online savings account). Next, set up automatic transfers from your checking account to your savings account. When you do this, set the transfer date to three to five days after your employer deposits your check. You don't want the transfer to go off when there are no fees in your checking account and attract overdraft fees. Ensure you also set the right amount to transfer to your savings account.

Next, log in to your savings account and link it back to your checking account. In my example, I would log in to my Emergency Fund and connect it with the Daily Transaction account. The reason you do this is to be able to transfer cash to your checking account in case of need. You can repeat the same process and link your checking account with your credit card to ensure you don't miss any payments. Of course, you may have more accounts. Simply follow this same logic to automate as many of your payments and savings as possible. Doing this allows you to spend only a few hours a month on money management.

8

THINGS TO AVOID WHEN SAVING

There are certain things that can financially pull you back while you're saving. Some of them look mundane but can cause severe financial disasters.

Take the story of this young woman, Eve, a 23-year-old retail employee. She had attempted to save several times but almost always failed to achieve her savings goal. At one time, she wanted to surprise her mom with a big birthday party and present. That was her financial goal and required her to go on saving mode. One day she was passing by a store and through the window, saw cute gold earrings, a beautiful neckpiece, and a matching watch. The moment she saw these gorgeous items, she felt the urge to buy them. She tried to avoid the feeling but eventually gave in and purchased the jewelry. And that action derailed her from achieving her savings goal.

The primary issue was that Eve had not yet become aware of the many actions that could kill off her financial dreams. Of course, she is not the only person who battles with reaching savings goals. And for most people, the issue lies with self-control. However, in some cases, it is the inability to handle emergencies intelligently that may be the problem.

This sad story is perhaps the kind that can cause you to pay attention to how you handle money issues so you can become a saver for good.

This is the story of Sam and Elsie. They fell in love and started a family that bore four sons. They worked hard to provide for their children. Elsie worked at a nursing home for 27 years, while Sam earned his living by hauling bags at the Kennedy and Newark international airports. Unfortunately, hard work took a toll on their bodies, and they both became disabled. However, the money they received from welfare, even after adding Elsie's pension money, could not support living in expensive New York City. So, they bought a Ford Windstar and a little ranch just north of Charleston and retired there.

Their financial problems began when they fell behind on their mortgage, and they discovered a financial product called a payday loan. We'll discuss this a lot more in a moment. They began taking on these kinds of loans. According to Wright (2011), at one point, Sam and Elsie owed as much as $3,800 two-week loans while their combined income was a mere $2,966. This means that the loan value was almost 130% of this couple's monthly income. What's worse is that these financially troubled parents had already taken twelve consecutive payday loans at the time. This is a cautionary tale about what could happen if you make certain mistakes as you save your money.

Let's now go over the specific actions to avoid if you want to reach your saving goal.

1. Avoid taking payday loans.

This is a big one. Payday loans are short-term credit advanced to you, expecting you to pay it in full in your next paycheck. They come in a variety of names such as "cash advance loans," "payday advance," or "salary loan." These loans often charge extremely high interest rates. They are easy to get because lenders frequently skip credit checks. Like in the story of Sam and Elsie above, you can easily borrow up over your monthly income. Most people take these loans to deal with short-term issues that may require quick cash they may not have.

It is easy to apply for a payday loan. All you do is provide your details, such as identification, banking, and residential details. As soon as your loan is approved, you get the money within 24 hours. You'll be required to pay back the loan in full plus interest once you get your next paycheck. This can actually make you dependent on these loans for a long time. If you struggle to pay for $300 of car repairs, how can you pay back $350? Anyway, at the time of application, the lender may ask you to sign documents that permit them to withdraw money from your bank account. These loans may feel like something you cannot avoid while you're facing a tight financial situation. I'll show you better alternatives before I finish discussing these loans.

There are certain groups of people that are targeted customers of payday loans. According to Livingston (n.d.), the following are prime targets for these loans in the US:

- **African-Americans**: African Americans are responsible for a quarter of payday loans despite forming just 12% of the American population.

- **Low-income people**: Households who earn less than $40,000 per year are three times more likely to use payday loans than those who make over $50,000.
- **Younger people**: There's a 50% chance that a payday loan user is aged between 20 and 44 years. On the other hand, the over 60s are less likely to become payday loan users.
- **The relatively uneducated people**: Over 50% of payday loan users haven't gone beyond high school, while less than 15% of these people have four-year degrees.
- **Separated or divorced**: People who are divorced or separated make up roughly 25% of payday loan users despite this population, making up just 13% of American adults.
- **Unemployed or disabled citizens**: As we saw with Sam and Elsie, payday loan lenders aren't shy to lend money against your disability or unemployment income. About 12% of disabled people have used payday loans in the past five years.

Why can payday loans be catastrophic to your

finances and stop you from saving? There are various reasons. For example:

- Payday loans come at exorbitant fees because they require you to make a once-off payment. For this reason, they can turn users into cash cows, and users can quickly become trapped in debt. Also, these loans can easily disorganize your monthly expenses due to the high charges, making it difficult to plan and stay on budget.
- When you take a payday loan, you give your lender the authority to take payments from your checking account, whether there's money or not. The danger with this is that if there's no money, your bank may charge you overdraft fees and make your financial situation intolerable.
- If you fail to repay the loan as agreed during your application, you may be forced to take another payday loan. Unfortunately, this leads to a cycle of debt that you'll find challenging to snap out of and may also tarnish your credit record.

The good thing is that there are alternative ways to

handle money emergencies that are not as expensive as payday loans.

- Aggressively build an emergency fund. This is where the discipline of saving comes. It doesn't matter how much money you save for this fund as long as you do. You may even find it easier to increase your contribution as your discipline grows.
- Pay some of your bills late. Some creditors will indeed add extra charges to your bill when you pay late. However, it is unlikely that they will add 40% and above for paying late. So, it may be a better move to pay some of your bills late to avoid paying colossal payday loan fees.
- Seek help. There are various programs that assist qualifying people with either food, utilities, health care, and even housing. For example, the Low Income Home Energy Assistance Program can help you meet your heating and cooling costs if you are a low-income earner.
- Sell items you may not need anymore. We've touched on this earlier in one of the chapters. This can be a great way if you

discover that your budget fails to meet your needs for a particular month. Again, you can see why budgeting is such an essential financial skill if you're to win your finance battles.

- You can borrow from friends or family. We've covered this option in detail earlier.

If you can, avoid taking payday loans and stay on track to achieve your savings goal. Otherwise, it may be ultra-easy to keep sabotaging not just your finances, but your overall life because you may develop the habit of failing to hit your goals.

2. Keep paying your credit card and other debts on time.

To save intelligently, it is better first to settle your credit card unless you're putting money away for emergencies. The reason is that credit cards often attract high interest rates that wipe out your net efforts of saving. But if you have chosen to keep paying your credit card, ensure you maintain your regular payments. You do this for countless reasons.

- The high interest rates quickly escalate your balance and make it difficult to settle the debt. Also, when you miss your payment, your credit card issuer may charge late fees that compound the problem.

- Your card issuer can sue you, or your account may be handed over to debt collectors. Unfortunately, this can result in a lower credit score and make it difficult to get credit with generous terms in the future.

If you happen to be persistently late on your payments, it may be an excellent time to review your budget and identify areas to reduce expenses. In some cases, it may be necessary to call your card issuer or your mortgage holder ahead of time and make payment arrangements. One great way of dealing with this situation is by creating another stream of income. As discussed earlier, freelancing has become one of the best ways to make additional money that can help you pay off your debts quicker.

3. Deal intelligently with the temptation to make unnecessary large purchases

Many people approach buying things in an emotional way. Of course, if you suggested to such a person that they buy with emotion rather than logic, they'd blatantly refuse. Yet, salespeople and copywriters know that the way to sell something to a buyer is to elicit a rush of dopamine, which can overcome the rational brain and get them to buy. Before you make large purchases, there are some things you can do to avoid being sucked into irrational buying. Let's talk about a few things you can do.

- Check if you have enough money to buy the item. If you find that you don't have enough to buy the item, avoid buying it until you're ready. Even if you have an emergency fund you can borrow from, the way to proceed is to avoid purchasing the thing. You want to showcase the right habits when dealing with money and temptations like this can derail your financial goals.
- Ask yourself if you genuinely need the item. Some people spend money on things they think they need without realizing that it is a matter of showing off or satisfying their luxurious taste. Unfortunately, habits like these can quickly pull you down financially. Just by asking yourself if you absolutely need the item, you're forced to activate your left brain thinking and start looking for

alternatives you may already have. In some cases, you may discover that you don't even need the item and can live without it.

- If you absolutely must buy the item, consider looking for a used one. In many cases, used goods are cheaper than new ones, and thus, you can save money. Even then, be mindful of the unplanned expense and possibly figure out a way to generate extra cash to buy it instead of using money from your regular paycheck. Perhaps you may even exchange something for the used item.

- Wait for the item to go on sale. Stores tend to place items that are slow movers on sale to get rid of them and improve their sales per square foot. This may be a good time for you to buy the item rather than when it's sold at its usual price.

One of the most potent ways to curb unnecessary spending on big items is to keep busy, preferably at home. Your focus determines where your energy goes. So, when you're focused on, say your gardening, there's no time to be thinking about buying that sofa you once saw at the mall. Because your focus is off the couch, it never occurs to you to buy it.

9

SAFER INVESTING FOR BEGINNERS

I t is well and good to save your hard-earned money in a savings account. The problem is that the returns are not as good, considering the impact of inflation. While saving is good, it serves only to get you to your financial goal in the short-term. What about if you want to have a lot more money when you retire or want to make a significant purchase in cash in the long-term? The tool to use to achieve a long-term financial goal is investing.

The challenge you may face with investing is that there's investment advice dished out in many media platforms, which may seem heaven-sent. However, if this were so, wouldn't a lot more people become wealthy? If the investment advice is good, why then do investment managers fail in numbers? Why do we have financial advisors who themselves aren't wealthy? Something must be wrong. But it is clear that trusting financial experts may not be the best thing to do to achieve your investment goals.

In 1986, the Financial Analyst Journal published a fascinating study penned by Gary Brinson, Randolph Hood, and Gilbert Beebower. These researchers wanted to investigate the impact of investment policy, market timing, and stock selection on the overall returns of an investment plan. Surprisingly, they discovered that marketing timing and stock selection were responsible for losses of 0.66% and 0.36% per year on an average portfolio. This means the noise we hear so often suggesting that investors buy particular stock or bonds does not necessarily work.

Investing is really about putting your money where it will grow the most over the shortest time possible without forgetting that by its nature, investing is a long-term game. Like any activity, investing requires you to have some elementary skills, and the way to learn those skills is by investing your time and energy in developing yourself. You're already on this path by reading and digesting the content in this book. The next important thing to do is to be convinced that you're the right person to invest your money. Who else cares about your money more than you do? Do you think investment managers would feel the same pain as you would if they lost your money in the market? Certainly not. So, it's vital to own up to your financial future. Perhaps this story illustrates the importance of taking responsibility for your finances and also shows you that you can make big money even if you're living paycheck to paycheck.

How a Working Woman Turned $5,000 into $22 million

Anne was an ordinary US citizen who joined the workforce when she was only 15 years old. She started as a bookkeeper. This woman thought that the best way to get ahead was to study. So, she enrolled in a night school at the predecessor of George Washington University Law School in Washington, DC. In 1920, she started to work for the Internal Revenue Services as an auditor.

At the age of 38, she began to invest in stocks using her life savings. At the time, she was earning about $3,000 a year, about $52,800 in today's value (DollarTimes, n.d.). You would think no one in her right mind would begin their investing journey when the

US was facing the Great Depression. But Anne had none of it. However, she trusted her 22-year-old brother Bernard enough to hand over her savings for him to invest through his brokerage employer. It seems as if things would work well as the market ticked up between 1933 and 1934. But then the brokerage firm that she had handed over her money collapsed, and she lost all her hard-earned cash.

Not to be denied, Anne began to save again with the aim of investing once more. For ten years, she stuck to her guns until she had saved $5,000. That was in 1944. She went to Merrill Lynch, Pierce Fenner & Beane, and opened an investment account. However, this time, she picked the stocks herself using her research skills and analytic reports from Merrill. Her belief was to buy shares of companies that were good and hold onto them for the long-term. Unsurprisingly, when she died in 1995, she had amassed $22 million, a return of 22% per year, not far from that of Warren Buffett of 22.7% (Thomason, 2005).

This story illustrates three critical points: First, take ownership of your financial future and be at the forefront of your investments. Secondly, if you're going to invest, do it for the long-term, that is, a period of at least ten years to mitigate market fluctuations. And lastly, an ordinary employee can make money on the stock market.

When Anne began her investing journey, a handful of companies were listed on the New York Stock Exchange (NYSE). But the NYSE has grown to almost 2,400 listed companies, making an intelligent selection of high-performance stock a mammoth task (Derjardins, 2017). There are better ways to do this, which we'll discuss in a moment.

When it comes to investing, the key is focusing on the things you have control over. The word 'control' is the most important in life and your finances.

ESSENTIALS OF SUCCESSFUL INVESTING

Four crucial elements go into successfully investing to achieve your financial goals. It is essential, therefore, to become aware and implement these important items in your investment strategy.

1. **Determine your investment goal**: Your investment objective answers why you're taking steps to grow your money. Do you want to have enough cash when you retire, or money for your kids to go to college?

Whatever your goal is, it's vital to be specific. Once you've determined your goal, you'll realize that there are certain limitations you may need to work with. For example, investment time available for you may just be 20 years, while for someone, it may be 30 years. Obviously, this will impact your choice of investment strategy and plan. The other factors to consider include, available funds to invest per year, and increases you'd want to make each year. If you approach investing with no plan, you are likely to pick the wrong strategy and suffer major financial losses.

2. **Asset allocation**: Once you have set your investment objective, you need to choose the kind of investment vehicles that would help you hit it. In this explanation, by asset class, I refer to stocks, bonds, and cash. According to a study by Scott et al. (2016), how you allocate investment assets determines your portfolio returns 91.1% of the time. Further, a diversified portfolio generally helps you mitigate unnecessary risk. If you were to invest only in stocks, you might expose yourself to high risk due to the volatile

nature of the individual shares. With a diversified portfolio, you try to balance risks and returns subject to your investment goal. Importantly, ensure your portfolio reflects diversity within an asset class as well as between asset classes. However, it is essential to rebalance your portfolio at least annually as the financial markets change to keep your investment goal on target.

3. **The cost of your investments**: Costs have a direct influence on the returns you get from your investments. The reason is simple to pick up. The expenses you pay radically reduce the amount of money that goes into purchasing your assets. This means you may buy fewer, and thus returns may be lower than if all funds had gone into the investment. So, consider all the elements that go into your costs, such as tax, management fees, trading charges, and so on, and minimize them. You can do this because, generally, costs are in your control.

4. **Develop and maintain self-control**: This is perhaps the most notable factor in the financial problems of sorts. Most people forget that the money game, like science, is

an intellectual sport. Instead, they allow their untrustworthy emotions to make buying and investment decisions. One of the reasons you need self-control is that professional investors try to time the market, and unfortunately, they consistently fail. And remember, professional investors have all sorts of advantages such as sophisticated tools, knowledge, skills, and access to other resources within their firms. But they still battle to time the market and beat it persistently. What about you who may be having far limited advantages? Your best weapon is self-control and diversification over the long-term.

What we have just discussed are the fundamental elements to seriously consider when investing, if you want to do it successfully.

WHAT TO INVEST IN

There are multiple options in which you can invest. Each has plusses as well as negatives. Further, each is good for specific kinds of investors. We can categorize your investment vehicles into lifestyle funds, index funds and mutual funds, and stocks, bonds, and cash. Let's briefly discuss each of these asset classes.

- **Stocks**: Stocks are nothing but instruments companies sell to raise funds to run the business. When you own company stock, you essentially own a portion of the business and may have a say in how the entity is run. Shares can either be ordinary (or common shares) or preferred shares. As a company shareholder, you qualify to receive dividends, which, if reinvested, can help you grow your investment quicker. However, stocks are highly volatile compared to instruments like bonds. Additionally, it is not easy to pick winning stocks regularly.
- **Bonds**: Bonds are essentially IOUs from governments and corporations. Unlike stocks, bonds offer you a known return that is available at maturity. However, they often deliver lower returns than stocks. The greatest advantage of bonds is that they are stable and, therefore, offer you low risk. As a result, bonds are a great candidate for conservative investors that are primarily

looking for security, not growth. It is for this reason that rich people often invest in bonds to protect their capital. But even then, putting $2 million on a bond that returns even 2% per annum still produces $40,000, money not to sneeze at. Bonds tend to perform well when stocks tank.

- **Cash**: Cash is essentially money that is currently uninvested. At best, the money is sitting in a savings account where it earns a meager return. In better situations, this money may be placed in a high-earning money-market account. The problem with cash is that over time it may be wiped out by inflation because it tends to grow at lower returns than inflation. Hence, you only want to keep enough to handle emergencies.

- **Lifestyle Funds**: Sometimes, these funds are called target-date funds. This is because lifestyle funds are used to achieve a specific financial goal at a dated future time. When you invest with this tool, you either focus on conservative, moderate, or aggressive risk. How much of a risk you can tolerate depends on your age. A dynamic approach suits younger investors, while older investors tend to vie for a conservative fund. It is a straightforward kind of investment to start and maintain. First, you don't have to worry about asset allocation because the fund is already diversified. Secondly, and most importantly, the fund automatically balances your asset allocation as you age. You don't have to spend an arm and leg on starting this fund as it requires only $1,000 to $3,000.

- **Mutual Funds**: Mutual funds are a pool of money collected from investors to invest in stocks and bonds, helping you manage risk. Investment managers are tasked with operating the fund so that it delivers good returns for the investors. The fund charges fees, called expense ratios, to provide its services. Most mutual funds are actively managed and therefore carry a higher risk. On the other hand, index funds are passively-managed. Essentially, these funds track the movement of a given market index such as the S&P 500. Sophisticated computers are used to follow the targeted index pattern of movement. So, index funds are cheaper than actively-managed mutual funds such as equity funds.

The information that I've provided you gives you an introduction to investment instruments. If you want to learn more about them, simply visit your favorite search engine, type your keyword, and begin exploring more.

HOW TO PURCHASE YOUR OWN INVESTMENTS

Now that you know the kinds of investment instruments you could start, let's talk about how to begin. Any type of investment begins with opening an account with either a brokerage house or your bank. The two most essential accounts for a beginner are the 401(K) and Roth investment retirement account (IRA).

The 401(K) Account

The 401(K) is a retirement account you get from your employer. The way it works is that you make automatic contributions regularly, usually monthly. Your employer may match your contribution up to a certain percentage of your annual income, such as

5%. If you want to optimize your investment into your 401(K), it is essential to contribute at least an amount that matches your employer's.

When you withdraw your money from a 401(K), you get taxed because your contributions are made with pre-tax income. You can choose specific investments within your account. The kinds of investments to add may include an assortment of mutual funds or target-date funds. Note that actively-managed mutual funds tend to be riskier. According to Kagan (2020), contributions to this account are limited to $19,500 per year for investors under 50, while the over 50s contributions are capped at $26,000 if there is no employer contribution. But when an employer contributes, investors under 50 are limited to contributing up to $57,000 or 100% of their annual paycheck, whichever is lower. On the other hand, over 50 years of age, people are limited to a yearly contribution of up to $63,500.

You are still responsible for selecting investment vehicles in your 410(K) account. If you want an easy instrument to invest with, I suggest you take the life-style fund based on your risk tolerance.

It is important to note that there's a set required minimum distribution (RMD) based on the Internal

Revenue Services (IRS) table. RMD is money that you must draw from your retirement account at a certain age, currently set at 72 (Kagan, 2020) in the US What if your employer does not offer you a 401(K) retirement fund? That's where the Roth IRA comes in. Even if your employer offers a 401(K), wouldn't you like to take ownership of your financial future or build a larger retirement nest egg?

Roth IRA Account

The Roth IRA made its debut in 1997 and is named after former Delaware Senator William Roth. This is an account squarely for individuals, and you build it with post-tax contributions that are not tax-deductible. For that reason, you are allowed to make tax-free withdrawals if you meet certain conditions. According to Segal (2020), you're not allowed to make contributions to Roth IRA if you make more than $139,000 a year or if a couple, more than $206,000. You are entitled to contribute up to $6000 per year if you're under 50 years old; otherwise, your contributions are capped at $7,000 per annum.

The good thing is that there is no minimum contribution and so it is easy to open and start this kind of account. You also benefit from the fact that you can keep the account open for as long as you wish.

Unlike the 401(K), there's no required minimum distribution. All the contributions you make must be from earned income.

Opening a Roth IRA account is easy and free. All you do is approach your bank and tell them that you want to open a retirement account, or research and work with a trusted brokerage house. In your research, ensure that you check the reputation of the brokerage and the fees they charge. Discount brokerage firms usually charge lower fees than full-service types. These days you're able to open Roth IRA accounts online. Once you've opened an account, your next step is to deposit the minimum account fee required to buy investments and then choose the kind of investment instruments that will help you achieve your objective. For a beginner, I suggest you purchase and regularly contribute to a lifestyle fund because it does automatic asset allocation and rebalancing. This allows you to focus on making regular contributions that you may automate the way I showed you in Chapter 7.

10

HOW TO STAY ON TOP OF YOUR FINANCIAL FUTURE

Your financial future is within your control. Yes, there may be challenges along the journey, but you have an asset that can help safely navigate and reach your financial destiny. The key to staying on track to achieve your future financial goals is your habits. What we habitually do determines the ki9nd of life we live. So, this chapter delves into the money habits to continually cultivate and practice to keep your finances in top shape.

1. Re-engineer your habitual focus

Most people who struggle financially focus on lack and limitation. The thing is that what we focus on grows. So, if you're focused on lack and limitation, you can expect a life of financial misery. That's not good at all. The way to solve this problem is to alter your focus and shine it on abundance and success. You're probably wondering, "how am I going to do it?" Don't worry; I'll show you in a moment. First, let me share an incredible story with a critical lesson on how to re-engineer your focus.

Patricia, a mother of two preschool children, faced insurmountable financial challenges when she got divorced. For starters, she had to keep paying school fees for her kids because her husband stopped paying child support. Moreover, she had her first and second mortgages to contend with, while her credit card was almost maxed out. Just these issues caused this woman sleepless nights. Despite her regular job and after-hours work, she still had a long month ahead after her money ran dry. She always spent everything that came in. It's not surprising that she was in perpetual struggle.

Realizing this, Patricia swallowed her pride and sought help. She consulted with an expert on how the mind works, specifically how the subconscious mind operates. The expert explained to her how the infinite intelligence within her could help solve her financial woes; then he offered her two simple words he knew worked for others in a similar situation. The words were wealth and success, and she was to use them as the foundation upon which to rebuild her financial life. He further told her to do an exercise every night just before she slept. This is what she had to do: prior to sleeping, she had to sit quietly, relax her body and mind and say, "Wealth. Success", in a slow manner but with feeling. He went on to tell her that she should do this exercise daily. I'm sure you'd agree that this is a simple example. Do not be deceived by its simplicity. Thomas Edison, the inventor of the incandescent light bulb, often practiced this exercise and got many of his ground-breaking ideas from his subconsciousness.

The subconscious mind is easily susceptible to suggestions just before you sleep and right after you wake up. The reason is that the conscious mind that guards the subconscious isn't highly active when you're drowsy.

This practice gave Patricia the chance to influence her subconscious mind, the seat of habits and emotions, and she did. One night while busy with this exercise, she noticed a vase that she had received from her aunt as an inheritance. On impulse, the following day, she wrote a description of the vase and posted it on an internet auction site. Within a few days, the vase was scooped up for over $7,000 (Murphy, 2001).

That sale began a new and exciting career for the once struggling Patricia. She regularly scoured yard sales for collectibles, which she would then sell at auction on the internet. Within 90 days, she was making more money than she ever got from both her regular and after-hours work. Without thinking twice about it, Patricia turned her new income stream into her regular job.

This story illustrates the importance of focusing on the right things. Patricia switched her regular focus from lack and limitation to abundance, wealth, and success. Soon, she began to see the opportunities she had previously ignored. I want to suggest you do the same exercise spelled above so your mindset changes from a poverty-set or middle-class to wealth-set. Using the words "Wealth. Success" is perfect because your current mental conditioning won't kick them out when you say them. This re-engineering process is most important to implement if you're to win your financial battles for good.

2. Cultivate the habit of paying yourself first

Paying yourself first has nothing to do with buying expensive suits, jewelry, or furniture for yourself. It means that, after getting your paycheck, your first step is to put away money for yourself. You can stash this money in a good savings account or invest it in your retirement account. The best way to do it is to automate the process, as explained in Chapter 7. It does not matter so much how much money you save regularly. What matters is developing the habit of saving.

Tom Corley, a certified public accountant (CPA), did research from 2004 to 2007 to find out what made people either rich or poor. In his study, Corley investigated the habits of 233 millionaires and 128 poor people. To his astonishment, he discovered that the rich lived by practices that were foreign to poor people. For example, he discovered that the rich save at least 10% of their gross income while the poor barely put away money. Kagan (2019), reports that few Americans ever save. For example, from 2016, less than 25% of Americans had enough savings to cover their six months of their monthly expenses, while 39% had no savings at all during 2017. That offers compelling proof that few Americans are wired to pay themselves first. Instead, they pay everyone, grocers, the taxman, etc., first and usually find that they have nothing to save (to pay themselves).

The top advantage of paying yourself first is that you begin to get your money to work for you. The power of compound interest will work for you and help you become financially secure much faster. Also, paying yourself first enables you to build an emergency fund that you can use to deal with unforeseen circumstances like paying major car repair bills or health bills.

3. Develop and nurture the habit of budgeting and reviewing your cash flows

We have already spoken at length about budgeting. The thing is that without budgeting, and reviewing your transactions, you have little chance of staying on top of your finances. You'll likely keep paying everybody but yourself. Between 2008 and 2014, I worked for a larger corporate firm and held a middle management role. One of my biggest tasks was to create an annual budget at a scheduled time of the year. For example, I created a 2012 budget towards the end of 2011, and it needed to be approved by various levels of the organization.

Once the budget was approved, it was my duty to ensure I did not overspend each month. This required that I review expenses weekly to catch any transactions likely to lead to overspending. I had to do this because the system was unforgiving. Someone else could spend your budget without your awareness, or your team could make unnecessary expenditures. When attending manager review meetings, you had to explain why you overspent, if you did, and give a plan to close the leaking hole in the following month.

You are like a business. So, you first must make a thorough budget to cover all the expenses you'll be making monthly. In this budget, all the income should be accounted for, and no dollars should remain. In other words, all the money should be allocated until the total income is equal to total expenditure. But don't stop here. Each month you should review your actual expenses and compare them with your budget. Where there's a difference, you should figure out why and make plans to close that gap in the following month.

Not only should you review your expenses: you should also examine the transactions on your bank statement. This way, you can catch any spending mistakes you may have made. You could also find out if your bank charges you excessive fees and potentially change to another bank.

One of the bad things about technological advancement is the spread of online theft. I remember there were times my checking account was debited monthly by some companies I didn't even know the existence of. These fraudulent transactions would stop after I blocked them at the bank, only to resurface after a few months. The unfortunate thing is that I could only know about these transactions if I studied my bank statements. So, do check your bank statements each month to ensure only transactions you've authorized go through in your bank account.

4. Cultivate the habit of frugality

What comes to your mind when you hear the word 'frugal?' To most people, being frugal means, you're cheap and stingy. That's far from the truth. If you look up the meaning of the word in your trusty dictionary, you'll immediately alter your perception. According to the Merriam Webster dictionary, frugality means "careful management of material resources and especially money." There you are. Nowhere does it say that when you're frugal, you are cheap. It is all about careful management of money, not wasteful. People who live lavish lifestyles are generally in the habit of hyper-consumption and waste a lot. You can even see this at the country level. Countries that are developed tend to produce more significant waste than poor and developing countries. And some of this waste can still be usable. Yes, big spenders may earn tons of money, but that doesn't mean they'll automatically become financially secure. They can play a great attacking game but with a leaky defense. They live what I call a high maintenance lifestyle that requires vast sums of money to sustain.

Fundamentally, when you are frugal, you live below your means. This means that you spend less than you earn. How do you do that? We've already highlighted some of the ways to do this throughout the book. The answer is that you need to watch how much you pay, which takes us back to budgeting. "Being frugal is the cornerstone of wealth-building" (Stanley & Danko, 1996, p.29). Stanley and Danko reached this conclusion after studying millionaires for about two decades. In the study, they also looked at what kind of purchases the millionaires made. One of their findings was that millionaires rarely bought any custom-made suits.

Here's what one the authors predict the millionaire studied would say if asked what's the most they ever spent on a suit, "The most I ever spent… the most I ever spent…including the suits I bought for myself and for my wife, June, and my sons, Buddy and Darryl, and my girls, Wyleen and Ginger…the most I ever spent was $399. Boy, I remember that it's the most I ever spent. It was for a particularly special occasion, our twenty-fifth wedding anniversary party" (Stanley & Danko, 1996, p.31). That's incredible, isn't it? But it is the answer most people would not have thought about and probably would disagree with. That would just be their perception, not necessarily reality. The kind of millionaires likely to buy custom-made suits were those who inherited wealth, not the self-made ones.

Social status is one of the things that guide people. Some believe their importance depends on how others view them. They live predominantly from the outside to inside. The self-image is the primary cause of this problem, and we discussed it in Chapter 2 above. There are a few practices you can habitually implement to begin to live frugally and maintain your finances under your firm control.

- First, define the kind of lifestyle you want to

live. This becomes your standard, and it must be the life you like and are happy with. When you do this, you avoid being influenced to live somebody else's life, which may be costly.

- Buy a used car instead of a new one. In the study I mentioned above, Stanley and Danko discovered that most of the millionaires they studied rarely bought new cars. Instead, they purchased pre-loved cars.

- Spend most of your time with frugal people. There's no doubt that our environment influences us. Just look at the kind of language you use. If you were born and raised in another country, would you be living the kind of life you do? Would you be eating the type of food you currently eat? Probably not. So, your environment counts. Make sure you are in the kind of situation that encourages the sort of money handler you want to become.

- When you buy things, try to buy the low-end brands. In many cases, you'll discover that the low-end brands are as good as the name brands. This is especially true when it comes to food and toiletries. When you buy such items, you immediately save money, which you can divert to your savings kitty. For significant items like furniture and appliances, it is wise to buy quality instead of going for price, to avoid frequent replacements in the future.

5. Develop the habit of reading

MJ Demarco had this to say about reading in his book *The Millionaire Fastlane*, "Education is free for your consumption. Infinite knowledge is at your fingertips, and the only thing preventing you from getting it is you. Yes, YOU. Turn off the TV, pick up a book, and read it. Quit playing Guitar Hero and hit the library. Quit playing Gameboy grab-ass and hit the books. A committed Fastlaner has his nose in a book weekly. He attends seminars. He trolls business forums. He's on Google, searching different topics and strategies" (DeMarco, 2011, p.238).

Unless you read books, you'll be more likely to be sucked into unproductive habits like binge-watching TV and programs that pull you back financially. Reading helps you widen your perspective about life and money. Over time, you'll begin to notice opportunities that may be hidden to those who don't flip the pages of a good book. Most rich people are readers, and they become and keep their wealth partly because they read. Join them, and your life will slowly but surely trend upward, especially financially.

You cannot have an enjoyable journey until you know exactly where you are headed. The same goes for your finances. You cannot achieve them until you know for sure what they are. In this book, I showed you that your first start to your financial health is to set your economic goals. Not only should you set the goals, but you should also write them down, burn them onto your mind and publicize them, so you commit to them. The way to burn your goals in your mind is to read them daily, at least just before you sleep and immediately when you wake up in the morning. This helps rewire your reticulating activating system, and it'll help you notice opportunities you may have been ignoring in the past.

You are not where you are financially by accident.

Your habits brought you to the situation you're in today. The main reason you're not yet financially secure is that you are predominantly a spender. To turn your financial situation around, therefore, you must adopt the spending behaviors of the tightwads.

Where do your habits come from? They come from many sources, including your school, parents, church, community, and so on. In Chapter 2, I showed you how to foster the kind of habits that'll help you save your hard-earned money. Yes, other people influence who you have become, but you are 100% responsible for changing yourself into the kind you wish to live like.

Your next important step, as suggested in Chapter 3, is to eliminate your debt. You cannot make financial progress while you are drowning in debt. It perpetually pulls you down. Before you can make serious progress on your savings journey, it's vital to eliminate debt, especially high-interest credit such as that of credit cards. I showed you how to create surplus money, such as starting side hustles and negotiating better deals to use to accelerate your debt repayment efforts. The faster you pay off your debt, the faster your savings will grow and will enable you to achieve your financial goals.

Chapter 4 covered the subject of credit cards in detail. We talked about the eight common kinds of credit cards available on the market. Credit cards are paramount because, when used rightly, they can help you handle emergencies and also offer you other advantages. However, they can be a menace when you haven't yet developed the habits of savers. Most importantly, we talked about your credit score and how it is calculated. Based on that, I showed you why you should focus on improving your payment history and the amounts you owe so you can boost your credit rating. Of course, if you don't want to apply to and use credit cards, you may loan money from friends and family. Treat these loans as if they're from a financial institution.

One of the most powerful habits to adopt to become an active money saver is to track your expenses. Why? When you follow your expenses, you'll quickly pick up areas where you can eliminate unnecessary spending. There are a variety of tools you can use to track your costs, such as spreadsheets and apps. Chapter 5 showed you what areas to focus on when eliminating unnecessary expenses. But to identify these areas, you must regularly draw a budget. Without a budget, you can spend money on unnecessary things. A budget is nothing but your spending plan.

Chapter 6 delved into how to reduce your costs on necessary items. We identified six areas where you can cut costs. For example, you can reduce costs by eating home-cooked meals instead of ordering from a restaurant. We shared with you research that proved that restaurant food is significantly more expensive than home-cooked meals. Other areas included cutting costs on entertainment, heating and cooling, refinancing your debts, and saving on transport.

Once you've created a budget, cut expenses on necessary and unnecessary items, and gotten your debts under control, you'll have surplus money every month. In Chapter 7, we talked about what you should do with that money. In fact, we suggested that you open a savings account, preferably an online savings account, because the yields are better than on a basic account. Which financial institution to choose for your savings account is a decision you must make based on your needs. But we went a step further and showed you how to automate your saving process to avoid missing some months.

As you start saving, there will be things that are likely to derail you. At the top is impulsive spending. If you have worked to adopt the habits of savers, this should not be a problem. Many people fall victim to payday loans, which cost them massive amounts of money. The reason for this is that payday loans charge high interests because they are short-term in nature. Do everything in your power to avoid them. Most importantly, while saving, ensure you pay all your debt to avoid incurring late fees and other charges.

Saving is excellent for short-term needs. For long-term financial needs, the best tool to use is investing. Notice that investing is not the same as trading. Investing is about growth, while trading is for quick income. There are many instruments or vehicles you can use for your investments, such as stocks, bonds, mutual funds, and lifestyle funds. In Chapter 9, we showed you why lifestyle funds are a better move for a beginner.

Most importantly, if your employer offers a matching 401(K) or a similar retirement account, enroll in it and begin to make monthly contributions. That's like getting free money from your employer towards your retirement. If there's no

401(K), immediately open a Roth IRA account and begin to invest for your future.

Finally, in Chapter 10, we talked about the behaviors to stick to so that you stay in control of your financial future. First, we talked about why you should re-engineer your habitual focus from lack and limitation to abundance and wealth. Then, we spoke about the importance of paying yourself first. This is important because most of us would rather pay tax first and then repay debt or creditors, and by the time we want to pay ourselves, we find there's no more money. We further discussed the reasons why you should regularly budget and then review your costs. This is the step even corporate managers don't practice in their homes but do at their workplaces. Most importantly, we showed why you should be frugal if you want to enjoy a bright financial future. We mentioned that frugality is not being cheap but economizing.

The message I want to leave with you as you finish reading this book is this: you are entirely responsible for your financial health. No one cares about your finances more than you do. So, take the lead and run them.

REFERENCES

AA. (n.d.). Easy Saver | AA. Www.Theaa.Com. https://www.theaa.com/savings-accounts/easy-saver

Bittencourt, T. (2017, December 7). Make money from your talents and skills: 7 amazing tips. Hotmart. https://blog.hotmart.com/en/making-money-from-your-talents/

Brinson, G. P., Hood, L. R., & Beebower, G. L. (1995). Determinants of Portfolio Performance. Financial Analysts Journal, 51(1), 133–138. https://doi.org/https://doi-org/10.2469/faj.v51.n1.1869

Calculate the value of $3,000 in 1932. How much is it worth today? (n.d.). Www.Dollartimes.Com. Retrieved June 3, 2020, from https://www.

dollartimes.com/inflation/inflation.php?amount= 3000&year=1932

Caldwell. (2019, June 25). Have You Used These 5 Budgeting Excuses? The Balance. https://www. thebalance.com/how-to-solve-budgeting-excuses-2385606

Chen, J. (2019, June 25). Lifestyle Fund. Investope-dia. https://www.investopedia.com/ terms/l/lifestylefund.asp

Compare Energy Prices | Cheapest Gas and Elec-tricity - uSwitch. (2000). USwitch; uSwitch. https:// www.uswitch.com/gas-electricity/

Covey, S. R. (2013). 7 Habits Of Highly Effective People. Simon & Schuster Ltd.

Demarco, M. J. (2011). The millionaire fastlane: crack the code to wealth and live rich for a lifetime! Viperion Publishing.

Desjardins, J. (2017, July 11). Here's the difference between the NASDAQ and NYSE. Business Insider. https://www.businessinsider.com/heres-the-difference-between-the-nasdaq-and-nyse-2017-7?IR=T

Easy Access Savings Account | Paragon Bank. (n.d.).

Www.Paragonbank.Co.Uk. Retrieved June 3, 2020, from https://www.paragonbank.co.uk/savings/easy-access-account

Eliminating unnecessary expenses - Wells Fargo. (2019). Wellsfargo.Com. https://www.wellsfargo.com/financial-education/basic-finances/financial-challenges/income/unnecessary-expenses/

Fay, B. (2012a). Credit Cards: Types of Debt & How Credit Cards Work. Debt.Org. https://www.debt.org/credit/cards/

Fay, B. (2012b). Family Loan Agreements: Lending Money to Family & Friends. Debt.Org. https://www.debt.org/credit/loans/friends-family/

Goldberg, M. (n.d.). Best Online Savings Accounts of May 2020 | Bankrate.com. Bankrate. Retrieved June 3, 2020, from https://www.bankrate.com/banking/savings/rates/#comenity

Hamm, T. (2015, May 18). 40 Ways to Save Money on Monthly Expenses. The Simple Dollar; TheSimpleDollar.com. https://www.thesimpledollar.com/save-money/trimming-the-fat-forty-ways-to-reduce-your-monthly-required-spending/

High-yield savings account. (n.d.). Sallie Mae.

Retrieved June 3, 2020, from https://www.salliemae.com/banking/high-yield-savings-account/

Irby, L. (2020, February 17). Here Is What Happens When You Make a Late Credit Card Payment. The Balance. https://www.thebalance.com/four-consequences-of-a-late-credit-card-payment-961070

Jespersen, C. (2017, February 14). 5 Steps for Tracking Your Expenses - NerdWallet. NerdWallet. https://www.nerdwallet.com/blog/finance/tracking-your-monthly-expenses/

Johnson, H. (2018, November). 11 Ways to Get Out of Debt Faster. The Simple Dollar; TheSimpleDollar.com. https://www.thesimpledollar.com/credit/manage-debt/11-ways-to-get-out-of-debt-faster/

Kagan, J. (2020). What is a 401(k) Plan? Investopedia. https://www.investopedia.com/terms/1/401kplan.asp

Kearns, S. (n.d.). The Psychology of Money - Saving and Spending Habits. https://www.moneycrashers.com/psychology-of-money-saving-spending-habits/

Learn About LED Lighting. (n.d.). Energystar.Gov.

https://www.energystar.gov/products/lighting_fans/light_bulbs/learn_about_led_bulbs

Lennox. (n.d.). Programmable Thermostat. Lennox. https://www.lennox.com/buyers-guide/guide-to-hvac/glossary/programmable-thermostat

Livingston, A. (n.d.). How Do Payday Loans Work? Dangers & Payday Loan Alternatives. Money Crashers. https://www.moneycrashers.com/how-do-payday-loans-work-dangers-payday-loan-alternatives/

Maltz, M. (2010). The magic power of self-image psychology: the new way to a bright, full life. Jaico Publishing House.

Mary. (2018, July 10). How Much Money Do You Save by Cooking at Home? - wellio. Wellio. http://www.getwellio.com/ranking-least-nutritious-meal-dollar-2/

Miller, T., & Yuko, E. (2019, October 22). What's the Best Temperature for My Water Heater? Lifehacker. https://lifehacker.com/whats-the-best-temperature-for-my-water-heater-1465372005

Murphy, J., & Mcmahan, I. (2001). Think yourself

rich: use the power of your subconscious mind to find true wealth. Reward Books.

MyFICO. (n.d.). What is a FICO Score and why is it important? | myFICO | myFICO. Www.Myfico.Com. https://www.myfico.com/credit-education/what-is-a-fico-score

National Credit Regulator. (n.d.). National Credit Regulator Annual Report 2017/18. Retrieved June 3, 2020, from https://nationalgovernment.co.za/entity_annual/1705/2018-national-credit-regulator-(ncr)-annual-report.pdf

Punjwani, M. (2019, March 15). Advantages and Disadvantages of Credit Cards by MoneySupermarket. @moneysupermkt. https://www.moneysupermarket.com/credit-cards/advantages-and-disadvantages/

Raab, G., Elger, C. E., Neuner, M., & Weber, B. (2011). A Neurological Study of Compulsive Buying Behaviour. Journal of Consumer Policy, 34(4), 401–413. https://doi.org/https://doi-org/10.1007/s10603-011-9168-3

Rick, S., Cryder, C., & Loewenstein, G. F. (2007). Tightwads and Spendthrifts. SSRN Electronic Journal. https://doi.org/https://doi-org/10.2139/ssrn.898080

Rudden, J. (2020, June 2). US personal saving rate monthly 2020. Statista. https://www.statista.com/statistics/246268/personal-savings-rate-in-the-united-states-by-month/

Schippers, M. C., Morisano, D., Locke, E. A., Scheepers, A. W. A., Latham, G. P., & de Jong, E. M. (2020). Writing about personal goals and plans regardless of goal type boosts academic performance. Contemporary Educational Psychology, 60, 101823. https://doi.org/https://doi-org/10.1016/j.cedpsych.2019.101823

Segal, T. (2019, April 30). Roth IRA Definition. Investopedia. https://www.investopedia.com/terms/r/rothira.asp

South African Reserve Bank. (n.d.). Quarterly Bulletin March 2019. South African Reserve Bank. https://www.resbank.co.za/Lists/News and Publications/Attachments/9148/01Full Quarterly Bulletin – March 2019.pdf

Stanley, T. J., & Danko, W. D. (1997). The Millionaire Next Door: The Surprising Secrets of America's Wealthy. Longstreet Press.

Sweet, E., Nandi, A., Adam, E. K., & McDade, T. W. (2013). The high price of debt: Household financial debt and its impact on mental and physical health. Social Science & Medicine, 91, 94–100. https://doi.org/https://doi-org/10.1016/j.socscimed.2013.05.009

Thomason, W. (2005). Make money work for you-instead of you working for it: lessons from a port-folio manager. John Wiley & Sons.

VanSomeren, L. (2019, September 13). How to Use a Credit Card to Build Credit: A Step-By-Step Guide. The Balance. https://www.thebalance.com/credit-card-build-credit-2385756

Wright, K. (2011, April 6). Bad Credit: How Payday Lenders Evade Regulation. Www.Thenation.Com. https://www.thenation.com/article/archive/bad-credit-how-payday-lenders-evade-regulation/

Yorkshire Building Society. (n.d.). Savings Account - More Information | YBS. Yorkshire Building Society. https://www.ybs.co.uk/savings/product.html